UNCONSCIOUS MENTAL LIFE AND REALITY

UNCONSCIOUS MENTAL LIFE AND REALITY

Edited by
Richard Ekins

Foreword by
Albert J. Solnit

Routledge
Taylor & Francis Group
LONDON AND NEW YORK

First published 2002 by Karnac Books Ltd.

Published 2018 by Routledge
2 Park Square, Milton Park, Abingdon, Oxon OX14 4RN
711 Third Avenue, New York, NY 10017, USA

Routledge is an imprint of the Taylor & Francis Group, an informa business

A subsidiary of Other Press LLC, New York

British Library Cataloguing in Publication Data

A C.I.P. for this book is available from the British Library

ISBN 9781855751972 (pbk)

Edited, designed, and produced by Communication Crafts

ACKNOWLEDGEMENTS

Thanks are due to Cesare Sacerdoti, to Wendy Saunderson of the University of Ulster, and to Klara Majthényi King of Communication Crafts for bringing this volume to final fruition. The quotations from Sigmund Freud (1900a), *The Interpretation of Dreams, Standard Edition, 4–5,* are reproduced by permission of A. W. Freud et al., by arrangement with Mark Paterson & Associates.

CONTENTS

CONTRIBUTORS ix

FOREWORD
Albert J. Solnit xi

Introduction
Richard Ekins 1

1 The distinctiveness of the psychoanalytic unconscious
Barry Opatow 19

2 What is affect?
Mark Solms 45

3 Mode of operation of unconscious mental processes as revealed by pathological forms of cognition
Thomas Freeman 83

4 Reflections on the psychoanalytic study of character
Clifford Yorke 95

5 Of teeth and theft and Poe:
non-Lacanian purloining
Ronnie Bailie 119

REFERENCES 137

INDEX 151

CONTRIBUTORS

RONNIE BAILIE is a psychoanalytic psychotherapist in private practice and Lecturer in English Literature at the University of Ulster at Jordanstown. He is the author of *The Fantastic Anatomist: A Psychoanalytic Study of Henry James* (1999) and is currently completing a book of psychoanalytic essays on St Paul, Shakespeare, Poe, Henry James, and Samuel Beckett.

RICHARD EKINS is a Member of the Contemporary Freudian Group of the British Psychoanalytical Society and Reader in Gender Relations at the University of Ulster at Coleraine, where he is Director of the Transgender Research Unit and Archive. His books include *Centres and Peripheries of Psychoanalysis* (co-edited with R. Freeman, 1994), *Blending Genders* (co-edited with D. King, 1996), *Male Femaling* (1997), and *Anna Freud: Selected Writings* (co-edited with R. Freeman, 1998).

THOMAS FREEMAN is an Honorary Member of the British Psychoanalytical Society. He was formerly Consultant Psychiatrist at the Anna Freud Centre, London, and at Holywell Hospital, Antrim,

Northern Ireland. He has published eight books and over 90 papers on aspects of psychoanalysis and psychiatry. His books include *Chronic Schizophrenia* (with J. Cameron and A. McGhie, 1958), *A Psychoanalytic Study of the Psychoses* (1973), *Childhood Psychopathology and Adult Psychoses* (1976), *The Psychoanalyst in Psychiatry* (1988), and *But Facts Exist* (1998).

Barry Opatow is a psychoanalyst in private practice and training and supervising analyst at New York University Psychoanalytic Institute, where he teaches basic Freudian theory to psychoanalytic candidates. He is also on the medical faculty of the State University of New York at Brooklyn, where he teaches psychoanalytic psychiatry to psychiatric resident physicians.

Mark Solms is an Associate Member of the British Psychoanalytical Society and an Honorary Member of the New York Psychoanalytic Society. He is an Honorary Lecturer in Neurosurgery at St Bartholomew's & the Royal London School of Medicine and a Lecturer in Psychology at University College London. His books include *A Moment of Transition* (co-edited with M. Saling, 1990), *The Neuropsychology of Dreams* (1997), and *Clinical Studies in Neuro-Psychoanalysis* (with K. Kaplan-Solms, 2000), and he is a co-editor of the new interdisciplinary journal *Neuro-Psychoanalysis* (with E. Nersessian).

Albert J. Solnit, formerly Sigmund Freud Professor of Psychoanalysis at the Hebrew University of Jerusalem and at University College London, is Sterling Professor, Emeritus (Paediatrics and Psychiatry) and Senior Research Scientist at the Child Study Center, School of Medicine, Yale University (New Haven, CT). Since 1991, he has been Commissioner of the Department of Mental Health and Addiction Services for the State of Connecticut (USA).

Clifford Yorke is a psychoanalyst in private practice and formerly Medical Director at the Anna Freud Centre, London, and a training and supervising analyst of the British Psychoanalytical Society. He has published widely on various aspects of classical psychoanalysis and is the author of *Development and Psychopathology* (with T. Freeman and S. Wiseberg, 1989).

FOREWORD

Albert J. Solnit

The power of Freud's discovery of psychoanalysis as a germinating centre for human psychology is firmly grasped and portrayed in this volume, the first of a series of three. The temptation to introduce yet another school of Freudian theory is firmly opposed in order to present a balanced view of Freud's thinking and that of his core group in Vienna and those who have succeeded them currently in what has been termed "classical psychoanalysis".

Elegantly and forcefully, this first volume documents and demonstrates the progressive vitality of classical psychoanalysis. It avoids the detours of trying to follow or encompass the fragmenting of psychoanalytic theory that characterizes many efforts to use part of Freud's thinking as a basis for a different or deviant approach. The emphasis here is on refining and adding to Freud's multifaceted work, not on replacing it. Also, in this volume there is the recognition that Freud's view could be modified, revised, and elaborated without obscuring the basic assumptions that became the foundation of Freudian or Classical psychoanalysis. As Ekins points out in the Introduction, an awareness of the origins of concepts that were repeatedly being revised and elaborated by Freud also gave rise to the hope that Freud's psychoanalysis could someday be the basis for a human general psychology. To a significant extent this book is an effort to avoid "a bewildering array of dissenting views and new schools" (Introduction) while providing a facilitating, unfinished view that connects current classical psychoanalysis to its origins.

There is a difference between allowing psychoanalytic theory to develop from systematic clinical observations and the risk of treating it as dogma. There is also the risk of splintering basic psychoanalytic presumptions into differing schools of thought that raise the spectre of different dogmas for different theoreticians and practitioners. This book is an effort to avoid dogma, following the unfolding, refinement, and revision of Freud's psychoanalysis, while being aware of the fundamentals of classical psychoanalytic theory. These fundamentals include an awareness of the unconscious, of how complex systems of dynamic economic, topographic, psychogenetic, and structural points of view are parts of the whole, and of how objectivity and subjectivity are not opposites, but different sides of the same person. It follows that there is an emerging view of how the functions of the mind and the brain can be related.

This volume, to be followed by at least two more, brings together seminal work that can be a repository of classical psychoanalysis, restoring and advancing the balancing focus and logical elaboration of Freud's legacy as extended by Anna Freud, Herman Nunberg, Heinz Hartmann, Ernst Kris, Robert Waelder, and many others of the second and third generations following in the footsteps of the Viennese group associated with the classical tradition of psychoanalysis. This contemporary series has been mobilized by our colleagues in Belfast, especially Richard Ekins, Thomas Freeman, and Ruth Freeman (see Ekins & Freeman, 1994; T. Freeman, 1988, 1998).

In preparing this volume, the editors and authors are guided by the bridging view that body and mind have a continuous mutual dependency and organizing influence on their respective functions. Chapter two, on affects, documents the classical psychoanalytic view of emotions as formulated by Freud, especially in his concept of drive theory. In addition, Solms relates recent neurophysiological research to Freud's concepts of the inner mind. Solms does this with the presumption that psychoanalysis, starting with Freud, has approximated the internal surface of consciousness, of the mind; whereas neurobiological approaches have studied the external surface of consciousness, of the mind. As Solms indicates, it is through the study of emotions that the inner and outer surfaces of consciousness can be compared and correlated.

Barry Opatow (chapter one) illuminates theoretically and clinically the shifting, multiple ways in which unconscious functioning reveals the complexity and principles of primary process in mentation, especially with regard to dreams and in affect development and expression.

These chapters set forth how classical psychoanalysis has unfolded and is currently viewed in its clinical and theoretical focus on the unconscious. Following these introductory chapters, there are three seminal examples of how updating classical psychoanalysis can illuminate "cognition" (Thomas Freeman), "character" (Clifford Yorke), and literary analysis (Ronnie Bailie).

Thomas Freeman describes in chapter three how the strategies and functions of the unconscious—where psychic reality exists—are manifested cognitively according to the different states of consciousness during normal and deviant conditions.

Yorke reminds us in chapter four that in classical analysis, as formulated by Anna Freud, there are three levels of conflict—that is, external, internalized, and internal—usefully invoked in the understanding of character. In this context object choice patterns are useful reflections of a signal aspect of character formation.

This first of three volumes enables those interested in classical psychoanalysis to use their own observations and experiences, clinical and non-clinical, in the continuing revolution of "understanding and expectations about human development and behavior" (Solnit, 1988, p. viii) that was created and set in motion by Sigmund Freud. Classical psychoanalysis is well prepared to respond to and to benefit from the complementary explanations that will emerge from the exchange between psychodynamic, biological, literary–artistic, and hermeneutic contributions. In the service of adding to our insights about human behaviour and development, this volume provides readers with the consolidating and focusing functions of classical Freudian psychoanalysis.

UNCONSCIOUS MENTAL LIFE AND REALITY

Introduction

Richard Ekins

As we enter the new millennium, it is evident that Freud's effort to establish and perpetuate a single, integrated science of psychoanalysis was a doomed enterprise. This should come as no surprise, when it is remembered that psychoanalysis is a bio-psycho-social science—in essence, a social psychology (Freud, 1921c, p. 69)—and that every social science has foundered in this respect. Just as contemporary academic psychology may be seen in terms of competing theoretical perspectives, variously biological, behaviourist, cognitive, psychodynamic, and humanist (Glassman, 1995), and contemporary sociology as made up of a plethora of perspectives variously positivist, interactionist, structural, and post-structural (Cuff, Sharrock, & Francis, 1998), so contemporary psychoanalysis is marked by an array of alternative and variously developed metapsychologies and theoretical perspectives, each with its own theories of mental functioning, of development, of pathogenesis, of treatment, and of cure (Wallerstein, 1988; Richards, 1998).

For a while, Freud and his followers were able to exclude from the ranks of psychoanalysis those who were seen as deviating from its fundamental premises—Carl Jung, Alfred Adler, and Wilhelm Stekel all left the psychoanalytic movement between 1910 and 1913, and Otto Rank followed in the next decade (Brome, 1967; Grosskurth, 1991). With Melanie Klein's entrance onto the psychoanalytic stage, however, this pattern was to change. From the mid-1920s onwards, Klein developed an alternative theory (Glover, 1945; Yorke, 1971, 1994) yet was careful to remain within the international body of accredited psychoanalysts—the International Psychoanalytical Association (IPA). She was able to do this when the "gentleman's agreement" within the British Psychoanalytical Society—following "The Freud–Klein Controversies" of 1941–45—created a tripartite structure within that IPA component society which perpetuated three separate training systems: Kleinian, "B" Group (later, Contemporary Freudian), and Middle Group or Independent (King & Steiner, 1995). The rest, as they say, is history. The Kleinian turn took root in geographical locations as diverse as Latin America, India, and Australia (Kutter, 1992, 1995), and the weight of emphasis in psychoanalysis in London gradually shifted towards Kleinian and object-relations theories and technique. Students and newly qualified analysts, most notably at the London Institute of Psychoanalysis, came to have little opportunity to familiarize themselves with the contributions of those authors experienced in the theoretical and technical concepts of Freud's psychoanalysis.

Meanwhile, in the United States, from the late 1940s on, ego psychology had become the dominant paradigm (Hale, 1995). While often depicted as "classical" and purporting to follow Freud, the ego psychologists—most notably Hartmann and his collaborators—in fact built upon highly selected aspects of Freud's corpus. As Sandler aptly put it:

> The ego psychological establishment in the United States (particularly in New York) maintained strict adherence to Freud's structural theory—the use of the topographical model was frowned upon—and developed it into a rather formal, some would even say rigid, system which placed much emphasis on the vicissitudes of mental energies, on the development of different aspects of the structural ego, and relatively little on life before the Oedipus complex. [Sandler, 1988, p. 8]

As the ego-psychological edifice began to fracture following the death of Hartmann in 1970, rather than returning to the older-style Freudian tradition the move was made towards ever newer developments—to Margaret Mahler (Mahler, Bergman, & Pine, 1975), Otto Kernberg (1975), and Roy Schafer (1976), in rapid succession; followed by a gradual importing of British Kleinianism and object-relations theory (Schafer, 1976). By the 1990s there was such a bewildering array of dissenting views and new schools that Wallerstein (1992), for instance, felt able to distinguish over a dozen separate approaches in a spectrum that included various American ego psychological, post-ego psychological, object-relational, Kleinian, Bionian, self-psychological, interpersonal, intersubjective, and Lacanian perspectives.

Such is the explosion of alternative approaches that we have now reached the position where knowledge of the original Freudian centre of psychoanalysis is in danger of being lost. Freud's psychoanalysis is not being taught or studied as a comprehensive body of theory and technique, either in the universities or in the psychoanalytic institutes (Yorke, 1992). In particular, the fact that Freud's psychoanalysis is, itself, a multi-dimensional approach that encompasses a number of models and points of view has given way to approaches that emphasize now this aspect, now that.

Freud's scrupulous attention to the "facts" of clinical observation led him repeatedly to revise his theoretical models and to add new models in order to embrace new clinical phenomena he confronted. For instance, in his final summary of his life's work, *An Outline of Psychoanalysis* (1940a), he maintains his allegiance both to the dynamic–economic theory of normal and pathological mental life that he first outlined in the seventh chapter of *The Interpretation of Dreams* (1900a) and to the structural model of the mind with its emphasis upon the importance of the ego and its objects, both internal and external, detailed most notably in *The Ego and the Id* (1923b). However, whereas Freud, himself, left it for his followers to "study all those functions equally" (of the psychic apparatus and its activities) (Freud, 1940a, p. 197), the various alternative approaches have developed selected aspects of his corpus, at the expense of other equally fundamental aspects. Thus, Lacanian analysis, for instance, quite deliberately excludes many of the contributions enabled by Freud's later structural model (Turkle, 1979), while the approaches of Klein and Fairbairn develop and extend the explanatory concepts introduced in Freud (1917e, 1920g, 1923b) and ignore almost entirely the contributions enabled by Freud's dynamic–economic theory (Freeman, 1998).

Thus does the need arise for publications that seek to bring about a revival of interest in Freud's psychoanalysis: in what may be identified as the "classical tradition in psychoanalysis". This volume is the first in a projected series designed to provide a focal point for those contemporary writers and practitioners working within the classical tradition. Following Couch (1995), we trace this tradition from the mainstream of psychoanalysis as it had been developed by Freud and his circle in Vienna and was later transmitted outside Vienna, through those members of the Vienna Psycho-Analytical Society who fled the National Socialists in the late 1930s and settled variously in Europe and America.[1]

Freud's circle in Vienna included a hierarchy of groups. There was the "old guard", who for the most part had belonged to the Vienna Psycho-Analytical Society before the First World War, including names such as Paul Federn, Theodor Reik, Hermann Nunberg, and Helene Deutsch. There was a second generation, who underwent a more or less systematic training which included a personal analysis. Anna Freud, Edward Bibring, Willi Hoffer, Heinz Hartmann, and Robert Waelder were prominent members of this sub-group. Finally, there was the group that trained formally following the inception of the Vienna Psychoanalytic Institute in 1925 and which included, amongst others, Richard Sterba, Annie Reich, Edith Buxbaum, and Ernst Kris (Leupold-Löwenthal, 1992, personal communication 1999; Sterba, 1982).

It was during this period, from the mid-1920s to the final break-up of the Society in 1938, following Nazi oppression, that an iden-

---

[1] See Jones, E. (n.d.) "Untitled document" (G07/BF/F01/01) and "Analysts Emigrated from Germany and Austria" (G07/BF/F01/02), Archives of the British Psychoanalytical Society. I am grateful to Jill Duncan, Executive Officer of the Library and Archives, British Psychoanalytical Society, for bringing these documents to my attention. See also the important Muhlleitner & Reichmayr (1997). See Lampl-de Groot (1980) on the contact between analysts in Vienna, Budapest, Prague, and—prior to 1933—Berlin, throughout what she refers to as the "second pioneer period" of the 1920s and 1930s.

tifiable Viennese "classical" tradition of psychoanalysis emerged. A number of factors, both theoretical and political, provided the impetus for the crystallization of this tradition at this particular time and place. First, between 1920 and 1926, Freud published a series of important revisions and additions to his corpus (Freud, 1920g, 1923b, 1926d), which called for major readjustments in psychoanalytic thinking. Freud's presence in the Society was felt as an inspiring force, and always Anna Freud provided a direct link to Freud when considering the ramifications of the revisions (Sterba, 1982). Second, by 1927, Freud's international "inner circle" of disciples charged with maintaining the purity of psychoanalysis finally disintegrated (Grosskurth, 1991).[2] Its place came to be taken by Freud's *"electi"* (Leupold-Löwenthal, 1992): a Vienna-based group of intimates whose importance grew steadily from the mid-1920s onwards. In the third place, from 1925 onwards, it became clear that a new deviation from Freud's view of psychoanalysis was looming in the form of Melanie Klein's new theories. In consequence, Freud felt he had to take further steps to ensure the realization of his own vision for the future development of psychoanalysis, particularly in the light of his ill health and possible pending death (Aguayo, 1997). I will expand each of these factors in turn.

During the early- and mid-1920s, Freud introduced three major new developments in psychoanalytic theory. Aggression as a drive in its own right was introduced in *Beyond the Pleasure Principle* (Freud, 1920g). A new structural model of the mind was detailed in *The Ego and the Id* (1923b). And the transformation theory of anxiety was replaced with the signal theory in *Inhibition, Symptom and Anxiety* (1926d). As Sterba recalls:

> This theoretical reversal (the new anxiety theory), the new structural model of mental anatomy, and the acknowledgement of aggression as a drive in its own right were three heavy impacts. They demanded fundamental changes in an analyst's theoretical thinking. These concepts profoundly increased our dynamic understanding while they brought about decisive changes in the therapeutic approach. [Sterba, 1982, p. 77]

---

[2] According to Muhlleitner & Reichmayr (1997, p. 80), the "Secret Committee" founded in 1913, which informally administered the International Psychoanalytical Association, was transformed into the official administration in 1927.

In short, Freud's followers were faced with the task of working through the significance of the new approaches for the further development of psychoanalysis, as well as for their own more personal theory and practice. This the Viennese analysts did, most notably in a number of important writings throughout the late 1920s and 1930s (A. Freud, 1936; Nunberg, 1931; Sterba, 1934; Waelder, 1936, 1937). These publications set the tone for subsequent developments within the classical tradition as that tradition extended throughout the world.

At the meetings of the Vienna Society, the group discussed Freud's most recent papers. As Sterba puts it:

> The closeness to Freud's work *in statu nascendi* gave us the feeling of participation in a major, future-shaping scientific and cultural process. Each new publication by Freud renewed and intensified this emotion and, since the Viennese analysts all shared in it, the feeling of belonging to a community of privileged individuals was unavoidable. This led to a sense of unity and harmony among the members. [Sterba, 1982, p. 81]

Furthermore, the younger Viennese analysts were greatly assisted in their understanding and absorption of the new ideas by their participation in the *Kinderseminar*—a study group for the younger members of the Society that met throughout the 1920s and 1930s. The various leaders of this technical seminar—Wilhelm Reich, Helene Deutsch, Hermann Nunberg, Edward Bibring, Grete Bibring, Richard Sterba, and, finally, Anna Freud—created an environment for the development of a coherent and cohesive tradition dedicated to "the cause": Freud's psychoanalysis. This Seminar was immensely important for the future stability and durability of the classical tradition.

Also of great significance was the fact that the early years of the Vienna Psychoanalytic Institute coincided with the final demise of Freud's "inner circle", which had previously been charged with setting the ground rules for psychoanalysis. Karl Abraham died in 1925; Otto Rank finally left psychoanalysis in 1926; relations with Sándor Ferenczi soured after 1927; and from 1926 onwards, Ernest Jones was increasingly preoccupied with championing Melanie Klein in London (Aguayo, 1997; Young-Bruehl, 1988). In replacing this disintegrating international group, Freud turned to his close-knit chosen group in Vienna to pass on the mantle of his own vision of psychoanalysis. This *"electi"* or "special group" was comprised of his daughter, Anna, together with his closest personal friends—Marie Bonaparte, Dorothy Burlingham, Ruth Mack-Brunswick, and, later, Jeanne Lampl-de Groot. Freud's first cancer operation, in 1923, led him to withdraw from regular attendance at scientific meetings, and from then onwards the *"electi"* was the only group that worked directly with him (Sterba, 1982).

Finally and most importantly, another split was emerging within the psychoanalytic movement. From 1925 onwards, Melanie Klein had been developing a psychoanalytic approach with children that collided, both theoretically and politically, with Sigmund and Anna Freud's interests (Aguayo, 1997). Anna Freud critiqued Melanie Klein in her "Introduction to the Technique of Child Analysis" (1927), but this was to be only an opening salvo in the long-running dispute with Klein. As Klein increasingly became the major thinker in the British Psychoanalytical Society, so Freud increasingly groomed his daughter to take over as his successor. Anna Freud, together with her group of colleagues in the Vienna Society, was particularly well placed to define the future development of psychoanalysis. She had her father's imprimatur and was one of the two leading players (with Klein) in the field of child analysis and in the psychoanalytic study of the child. Furthermore, her rapid rise to power within the Viennese Psycho-Analytical Society, throughout the late 1920s and 1930s, coincided with the Society's "exceptional golden age" (Leupold-Löwenthal, 1992).

Taken together, these factors set the tone for the establishment of a distinctive Viennese tradition of psychoanalysis, now identifiable as the Classical tradition. Following their enforced emigration, mainly to England and America, members of this group duly transmitted their approach to new generations of trainees, thus enabling Couch (1995) to depict "classical" psychoanalysis as referring to "the body of theoretical contributions and personal technique of Freud and his close colleagues in Vienna who later emigrated to England and America before the Second World War" (Couch, 1995, p. 153).

Unlike those traditions that have developed from particular points in Freud's corpus or particular perceived hiatuses, the "Classical tradition" takes as its lift-off point the whole body of

Freud's work while embracing the many Freudian contributions since the 1930s. The major hallmark—perhaps *the* distinctive feature of this classical tradition—is that of "balance". In a number of papers Couch (1995, 1997, 1999) has consolidated the central features of classical technique. Classical technique pursues "a *balanced* focus on interpretations of transference, resistance, dreams, memories, past and current relationships, character, defences and developmental reconstructions" (Couch, 1997, p. 1). It does so in the spirit of technique following theory. As we have seen, the major early names in this tradition—Anna Freud, Edward Bibring, Willi Hoffer, Robert Waelder, Richard Sterba—were initiated into psychoanalysis at the time when Freud introduced his structural model. They accepted the new model as an addition to, rather than as a replacement for, the existing body of Freud's contributions. As Anna Freud was to put it later:

> Different from the people who found the structural theory existing when they entered psychoanalysis and saw the topographical scheme as a thing of the past, I grew up with the topographical scheme, and had a gradual transition to the structural in my own psychoanalytic development. I must say that in my writing I never made the sharp distinction between the two that later writers made, but according to my own convenience I used the one or the other frame of reference. I definitely belong to the people who feel free to fall back on the topographical aspects whenever convenient, and to leave them aside and to speak purely structurally when that is convenient. [Sandler with A. Freud, 1985, p. 31]

This balanced approach is a direct corollary of a commitment to the classical Freudian metapsychology, whether it be phrased in terms of classical psychoanalysis as a multi-model system of dynamic, economic, topographic, psychogenetic, and structural points of view (Noy, 1977) or, in terms of the fundamental "discoveries" and formulations of classical psychoanalysis listed by Anna Freud as

> the sequence of libidinal stages as the normal precursor of mature sexuality; the ubiquity of the Oedipus and castration complexes; the legitimacy of narcissism as a forerunner of and adjunct to object love; the developmental stages of the ego

> with its mechanisms, functions, and contents; the stages of the aggressive drive; and the overriding general impact of the mother–infant relationship, etc. [A. Freud, 1974, pp. 61–62]

As Couch explains:

> Behind classical technique lies Freud's metapsychology of the well-known conceptions of instinctual drives and ego defences, infantile sexuality, psychic energy, mental structure of id–ego–superego, topographical levels of unconscious, preconscious and unconscious thinking, developmental origins of disturbances, a theory of dream and symptom formation and of mental functioning as a dynamic interaction of unconscious forces. [Couch, 1997, p. 3]

If to these we add emphasis to the importance of the body, the psycho-physical theory of mind, the importance of the pleasure principle, the distinction between primary process and secondary process thinking, infantile amnesia, the repetition compulsion as an irreducible element of mental life, the emphasis on the observable, and the overriding importance of the developmental point of view (anti-essentialism), we can see something of the richness of the classical tradition and how much of it is in danger of being lost in the current focus on ever more alternative formulations, or on the developing of increasingly limited aspects of Freud's oeuvre.

In choosing a theme for this first volume, I was mindful of the fact that what unites all psychoanalytic approaches is the focus on unconscious mental processes and, further, that in all of Freud's attempts to explore the nature of unconscious mental processes, questions of the nature of and significance of "reality" loom large. Wallerstein (1995) provides an excellent review of the development of Freud's conceptualizations of reality. As Wallerstein outlines, initially Freud (1950 [1895], p. 373) distinguishes "thought reality" from "external reality", without definition. In Freud (1900a, p. 613) "thought reality" becomes "psychic reality", and in Freud (1912–1913, p. 159) "psychical reality" is counterpoised to "factual reality". In his 1919 edition of *The Interpretation of Dreams,* "factual reality" becomes "material reality", and the final form of the relevant sentence becomes: "If we look at unconscious wishes reduced to their most fundamental and truest shape, we shall have to conclude, no doubt, that *psychic* reality is a particular form of existence not to be confused with material reality" (p. 620). Throughout his corpus, Freud is continually preoccupied with the nature of psychic reality and its relations to unconscious and conscious mental processes (the internal world) and to material reality (the external world).

With my theme chosen, the task then became to select important contemporary exponents of the classical tradition to cover the range of major issues presupposed by Freud's "balanced" approach to problems of unconscious mental life and reality. The neglect of the contemporary significance of Freud's psychophysical and dynamic–economic theory by all the major alternative traditions in psychoanalysis made it particularly important to include works that focus on this aspect of Freud's corpus. Chapters one to three are all rooted very explicitly within the dynamic–economic theory. The contemporary neglect of the significance of external reality ("real events"), particularly in Kleinian and Lacanian analysis, led to my seeking contributions emphasizing this aspect of the classical tradition. Consideration of the impact and importance of "real events" provides a partial focus for chapters three and four, and the particular focus of chapter five. I should also add that when soliciting manuscripts, I asked each contributor what the "classical tradition in psychoanalysis" meant to them and how they saw their own work, past, present, and future, fitting in with this tradition. I have drawn on this material in some of the comment that follows.

In chapter one, Barry Opatow returns to Freud's topographical model of the mind to present a subtle and persuasive rendition of the distinctiveness of the psychoanalytic unconscious, valuable to contemporary analysts seeking a rapprochement with the cognitive revolution in the sciences. Whereas Freud was able to contrast his own creation of a depth psychology—a psychology of unconscious mental processes—with the psychology of consciousness (and later of behaviour), the contemporary turn in psychology has seen an increasing acceptance of and turn to unconscious mental processes (Erdelyi, 1985; Shevrin, Bond, Brakel, Hertel, & Williams, 1996). However, modern developments in the psychological sciences outside psychoanalysis lack a satisfactory fusion of "desire" with "cognition". Here Opatow finds the need to return to Freud to provide the foundations for a psychoanalytically serviceable conception with which to meet the "cognitive turn".

For Opatow, inquiries into hallucinatory wish-fulfilment and unconscious mental life converge and, by distinguishing the concept of the unconscious in psychoanalysis from that of cognitive psychology, serve to bring out what is most essential to the psychoanalytic conceptualization. Opatow uses Freud's topographical model to stress that the psychoanalytic unconscious can be understood only in relation to theories of consciousness and wishing. Moreover, in contrast to the cognitive conception, psychoanalysis holds that the processing of thought in the human mind is inseparable from the activity of desire. This leads Opatow to further reflections on the interrelations between conscious and unconscious, wishing and thinking, and, in consequence, on transference and the mechanisms of unconscious fantasy.

Placing the focus on unconscious mental life and "reality", we see Opatow detailing how the inherent dynamism of unconscious wishes—the primary process—presses towards hallucinatory wish-fulfilment, both grounding the concept of psychic reality and making possible the efficacy of unconscious fantasies. He provides a phenomenological analysis of hallucinated satisfaction, thereby demonstrating how the mind, through purely internal operations, generates an experienced reality. His major thesis is that the psychic reality of the dynamic unconscious is continuously grounded in the subjective reality of hallucinated satisfaction. Opatow shows how the two separate categories of *reality*—the material and the psychic—are rooted, respectively, in external perception and hallucinatory belief, demanding two kinds of thinking to apprehend them, corresponding to Freud's primary and secondary processes.

Opatow regards himself as an exponent of the "classical tradition" primarily with regard to the contribution that psychoanalysis can make to the study of the human condition and the theory of the mind. He asks: "How is it that the most fruitful meeting ground of modern neuroscience and psychoanalysis is widely regarded as Freud's original metapsychology? (The Project). It is sensed that, possibly, here lies an abstractive intensity to bridge these logically distinct domains" (Opatow, personal communication). Opatow's interests in the significance of Freud for the interrelations between phenomenological philosophy, cognitive psychology, and neuroscience have led him to value the work of Mark Solms, who for a number of years has been exploring the significance of Freud's work for contemporary neuroscience. While it had long been fashionable to dismiss Freud's metapsychologies of mind and body as being based on inaccurate and outmoded nineteenth-century notions, Solms has made it his task to show just how in tune Freud's formulations are with contemporary neuroscience and to develop these formulations in the light of modern research programmes (Solms, 1995b, 1997a). In chapter two, Solms considers Freud's metapsychological formulation of affect in the light of contemporary neuroscience. He argues that the problem of affect—perhaps more than any other—forces us to acknowledge the intrinsic connection between mind and body, and to accommodate it in our theoretical formulations. Solms's review of the problem from this point of view leads to the formulation that affect is a primary sensory modality, analogous to the senses of vision, hearing, somatic sensation, taste, and smell. These modalities are the elementary constituents of the envelope of consciousness, from which it is impossible to free ourselves. Whereas the sensory modalities of vision, hearing, somatic sensation, taste, and smell represent aspects of the external world of objects ("unknowable" in themselves), affect is the primary sensory modality through which we perceive an aspect of the internal world of the subject (unconscious in itself).

Solms points to the neglect of the psycho-physical by other traditions in psychoanalysis. He emphasizes that physical and psychic perceptions—the perceptual data of consciousness—must be the starting point for all research. Psychoanalysts study reality from the viewpoint of the *internal* surface of consciousness. Accordingly, the object of psychoanalytic research is that aspect of reality which determines introspective consciousness. Solms also reviews Freud's detailed justification for describing this aspect of reality in *psychic* terms and his arguments for establishing psychoanalysis as a science of psychic reality, referring to the unconscious reality within us, when it is considered from the viewpoint of subjective awareness.

Turning specifically to affect, Solms argues that since affect is the primary sensory modality through which we perceive the internal (subjective) world of psychic reality, it follows that just as the external senses represent aspects of reality to us in the form of sights, sounds, bodily sensations, tastes, and smells, so our internal sense organs represent an aspect of reality to us in the form of emotions. Moreover, just as each external sensory modality represents reality in the form of a particular qualitative range (e.g. the wavelength composition of light), so, too, the sense of affect has its own qualitative range. We conventionally calibrate this range in terms of relative degrees of pleasure and unpleasure. We may therefore consider pleasure and unpleasure to be the basic qualities of the sensory modality called affect. Solms then provides a valuable overview of the physical correlates of affect and of its metapsychology, indicating the need to test our metapsychological inferences against empirical data, by means of original research undertaken specifically for the purpose.

While Opatow and Solms (in New York and London, respectively) represent a younger generation of workers within the Classical tradition of psychoanalysis, in chapters three and four we turn to the work of Thomas Freeman and Clifford Yorke, two "elder statesmen" of the classical tradition in the United Kingdom. Both Freeman and Yorke worked with Anna Freud (and her close colleague Dorothy Burlingham) for almost three decades, until Miss Freud's death in 1982. They have both proven to be exceptional standard bearers of the classical tradition, Freeman through his work with psychotic patients and with students of the Northern Ireland Association for the Study of Psychoanalysis (NIASP), and Yorke through his work with children at the Anna Freud Centre and with students of psychoanalysis at both the London Institute of Psychoanalysis and the Anna Freud Centre.

Thomas Freeman's extensive experience with the functional psychoses (the schizophrenias and maniacal psychoses) before the advent of chemotherapeutic agents rendered him particularly sensitive to the value of Freud's topographical model as detailed in Freud (1900a). In particular, Freeman demonstrates how pathological forms of cognition and the dreams of the healthy and neurotically afflicted reveal the mode of action of unconscious mental processes: Freud's primary process. Freeman details the perseverations and substitutions that substitute for rational thought, the perceptual anomalies, and the disturbances of memory occurring in the schizophrenias, and organic mental states. Observation of cases of chronic brain syndrome suggests to Freeman that transitivism arises initially as a result of psychic dissolution alone and only secondarily becomes involved in mental conflict. Further, he emphasizes that whilst primary and secondary thought processes may be distinct conceptually, in practice they are to be observed in concert, the balance of their interrelations depending upon the different type of cognitive organization currently in the foreground.

Freeman's particular concern is "delusional reality". Through close long-term observation of the behaviour and utterances of psychotic patients, Freeman is able to map the mode of activity of primary process thought revealed when psychic dissolution brings about pathological forms of cognition. He demonstrates how pathological forms of cognition take the place of goal-directed, abstract thinking and a veridical representation of reality, and how with psychic dissolution the hierarchical inhibition of lower by higher modes of mental activity is reversed. Throughout his chapter, Freeman is careful to confine himself to the empirical data and notes that the phenomena that reflect the action of the primary process offer nothing about the nature of unconscious processes themselves. For Freeman, as for Freud (1900a), "The unconscious is the true psychical reality; in its innermost nature it is as much unknown to us as the reality of the external world by the communications of our sense organs."

To Freeman, "classical psychoanalysis" is simply "Freud's psychoanalysis". Initiated into the tradition by his teachers Dorothy Burlingham, Anna Freud, and Willi Hoffer, who all saw themselves as transmitting the Freudian legacy and working within it, he sees no need to identify with any other thinker or school. In particular, he identifies with the tradition of empirical clinical observation introduced by Freud in his earliest psychoanalytic papers (Freud, 1893a, 1894a, 1895c) and set forth in greater detail in *Studies on Hysteria* (Freud, 1895d). Clifford Yorke takes a slightly different position. After years of working with Anna Freud, Yorke became a staunch Anna Freudian as well as a Freudian. He found that child analysis deepened his convictions about Freud's psychology, and for him psychoanalysis rests on basic Freudian principles, their enlargement and extension through Anna Freud and child analysis, and the many important contributions from others extending that line of development.

In chapter four, Yorke provides a comprehensive review of the contribution of the classical tradition to the psychoanalytic study of character and sets forth a number of directions for further research. Freud was concerned with a libidinal sequence in which innate "givens" unfolded under the influence of experience. Yorke argues that if we think in terms of oral, anal, and phallic organizations, a sequence of the effects of drive derivatives and defences against them is still of some validity. But we encounter difficulties when, for example, we think of "strong" and "weak" characters and ask ourselves what libidinal correlates can be found for them. He explores how the differentiation of character *traits* and character *structure* illuminates classificatory systems. Further, in accordance with the classical tradition's empirical approach, he argues for attention to description and the phenomenology of character, understood psychoanalytically. For Yorke, a psychoanalytic view of character has to be understood developmentally, notwithstanding the immense difficulties likely to be encountered in any sustained examination of character along these lines. Yorke's developmental approach takes into account the adaptive as well as the maladaptive character and considers the role played in all this by ego and superego development as well as changing drive organization. His treatment of masculinity and femininity within the individual pays the proper respect to the complexities of the Freudian position in this area. In a final section, Yorke introduces the topic of the open and closed personality, with emphasis on the repression barrier and its relationship to ego and superego development.

Yorke's consideration of the importance of reality and "real events" builds upon Anna Freud's distinction between external conflict, internalized conflict, and internal conflict when he argues that a comprehensive treatment of character presupposes a detailed and systematic consideration of the interrelations between external reality, reality that was once external but has become part of a person's internal world, and that part of the person's internal world consisting of inborn tendencies, such as activity or passivity, masculinity or femininity. Furthermore, by considering the relationship of the internal agencies of id, ego, and superego to each other as well as to the outside world, the path is cleared for a possible metapsychology of character.

In the final chapter, Ronnie Bailie turns to the topic of psychoanalysis as applied to literature. For Bailie, the classical tradition (embodied in Freud himself and the first generations of analysts) achieved a great deal in theoretical and clinical work but did little applied work of commensurate stature. The core insight (and the most productive one, potentially) was the analogy of the work of art to the dream. Bailie is concerned with the untapped potential in early psychoanalysis and is opposed to the ego-psychological position, which emphasizes the element of ego mastery in the act of creation. For Bailie, the artist neither chooses nor controls in a conscious or deliberate way. As he sees it:

> He may have the subjective impression that he does and he may engage in activities that seem to confirm his control: really the "secondary revision" of the dream-work and already a kind of commentary, something after the fact. You no more choose what to write than you choose what to dream. [Bailie, personal communication 1999]

Bailie's chapter highlights how even the highest cultural products are infantile in origin and result from the transformation of instinct. Turning to the specific content of Bailie's chapter, we find him focusing his arguments on the concrete reality of the idea of theft in Edgar Allan Poe's life and work. Paying particular attention to the "facts" of Poe's early upbringing—the ambivalence of John Allan's "giving", Poe's unconscious memories of his mother's terminal illness, and the increasing prominence of her teeth as she wasted away with consumption—Bailie links these "real events" to the oral phase of libidinal development and to Poe's oral sadism, as he meticulously sets forth the determinants that explain why so much of Poe's psychic energy was caught up in the issue of theft. In particular, Bailie's reading of *Berenice* and *The Purloined Letter* provides convincing arguments that, for Poe, the Gothic literary repertoire provided convenient masquerades in which he could present his core realities as if they were a series of fabrications.

Thus does each chapter pay the proper respect to the range of Freud's thinking on unconscious mental life and reality. Opatow's focus is on the "real unconscious" and psychoanalysis as a theory of consciousness. Solms provides an impressive argument that a theory of affect founded upon Freud's metapsychology provides the much sought-after "missing link" between the mind and the body, between internal and external reality. Freeman emphasizes the importance of Freud's earlier work if the delusional reality of schizophrenic patients is to be understood. For Yorke, any adequate treatment of character must pay full attention to the interrelations between internal, internalized, and external reality viewed developmentally over the life course. Finally, in Bailie, the impact of external reality and "real events" set in the context of libidinal development are given particular significance. Taken as a whole, these contributions in the classical tradition provide a fitting tribute to the legacy of Freud's psychoanalysis—its depth, range, balance, and continuing vitality and relevance for the new millennium.

CHAPTER ONE

The distinctiveness of the psychoanalytic unconscious

Barry Opatow

This chapter mines the conceptual resources of classical metapsychological theory, especially its most trenchant and dynamic exposition in the final chapter of *The Interpretation of Dreams* (Freud, 1900a), for its singular contribution to a basic theory of human consciousness. Metapsychology's fundamental postulate of mind embodied in a sentient organism struggling to survive suggests a deep-lying genetic unity of the mind's prime motivational, affective, and cognitive activities. This brings into focus the interrelations of desire (and need) to the psychogenesis

This chapter is an adaptation of work on two panels of the American Psychoanalytic Association, New York City, 15–16 December 1995: "Hallucinatory Wish Fulfilment", J. Kite (chair), A. Bass, D. Moss, B. Opatow, G. Fogel (discussant); and "The Couch, the Laboratory, and the Brain: The Unconscious", H. Shevrin (chair), B. Libet (neuroscience), P. Merikle (cognitive psychology), B. Opatow (psychoanalysis), O. Flanagan (philosophy: discussant). The author is grateful for the editorial assistance of Alan Bass, Howard Shevrin, and William I. Grossman. An earlier version of this chapter first appeared as "The Real Unconscious: Psychoanalysis as a Theory of Consciousness", *Journal of the American Psychoanalytic Association, 45* (1997): 865–890 (reprinted with permission).

of objective, experiential reality and, therefore, to the structure of thought in general. In particular, I will try to show how his vital interdependence of thought on reality—and, further, of both on desire—implies the formulation of the psychoanalytic unconscious as a structure of human consciousness.

To endure recognizably as a basic theory, its essence undestroyed, psychoanalysis must, more than most scientific activities, withstand, absorb, and transcend the tidal wave of the "cognitive revolution" immersing all of science and technology. Even physics is not immune, having to cope with the allegation, intended seriously, that the universe is a cosmic algorithm. At stake is whether the informational and neural sciences have at their disposal conceptual resources of sufficient descriptive reach and explanatory force to encompass fully the main theoretical problems of mind—especially those of subjective experience, motivation, and thought—and thus eliminate psychoanalysis as a *basic* theory altogether. This situation demands inquiry into what is truly essential to the foundations of basic psychoanalytic theory.

We have no unified notion of the unconscious, even within psychoanalysis itself. This is evident when one considers that the concept of the unconscious is virtually coextensive with psychoanalysis as a whole, and that this whole divides into several separate schools. Does the unconscious comprise sexual drive derivatives, internal object relations, or narcissistic needs? As this diversity of psychoanalytic schools emanates from a common source in Freud, I will try to extract the formal essence of the Freudian theory of the unconscious in the hope of providing a prototype on which all of psychoanalytic theory can re-converge. My aim is to generate a representative point of view that can engage the other sciences. To be sure, my account of Freud is selective. I choose to emphasize the topographical theory because of its particular importance for the theory of consciousness and thought—topics of current interest in the cognitive and neural sciences.

This methodology does not abjure the structural theory but, in fact, implicitly endorses and promotes it. I agree with Ernst Kris, Kurt Eissler, and especially Hans Loewald (1966) that topographical concepts are crucial for conceptualizing the mental processes forming the psychic structures that enter into conflict. (For my attempt explicitly to integrate topography and structure, see Opatow, 1993; note also Solms's, 1995b, confirmation of topographical metapsychology in cutting-edge neuro-psychological research.

With respect to method, it is evident that the theorizing in this chapter, apart from a single vignette, proceeds at a far remove from observational data. This is often the case in attempts to formulate a truly basic level of scientific theory, the prime example being Einstein's indifference to experiments as he forged relativity out of an "unbearable" asymmetry in Maxwell's equations (Holton, 1988). Here I take existing theory as my primary datum. I try to operate on this theory to reach an abstractive intensity in which many psychoanalytic propositions can be unified.

Freud (1900a) first presented a comprehensive theory of the unconscious to account for the interrelations of symptoms and dreams. Implications crucial for the concept of the psychoanalytic unconscious follow from this integration. The clinical hypothesis that a dream not only indicates or represents the existence of an unconscious wish but can also *fulfil* it provides the basis for the radical formulation that *satisfaction can be hallucinated.* Further, an inherent dynamism of unconscious wishes—the primary process—presses towards such hallucinatory actualization (p. 602). I want first to show that this thesis of hallucinatory wish-fulfilment both grounds the concept of psychic reality and makes possible the efficacy of unconscious fantasies. The discovery of the latter was the scientific anomaly that gave rise to psychoanalysis. Then I wish to show that unconscious fantasy is integral to any comprehensive theory of cognition, in order to demonstrate why psychoanalytic theory can answer questions that cognitive psychology cannot.

Hallucination and fantasy

Hallucinatory wish-fulfilment is in several respects a foundational concept for psychoanalysis. Indeed, its explication is not merely an inquiry into a peculiarly fascinating hypothesis. Rather, it opens out into questions that pertain to the nature of psychoanalytic theory as a whole—how it defines itself, its object, and its limitations and relations to the other mental sciences. In this sense, the fluctuating status of this concept within our field may function as an index of how psychoanalysis views itself at a given time.

The concept of hallucinatory wish-fulfilment is, in the first place, historically fundamental. It was formally introduced by Freud in chapter 7 of *The Interpretation of Dreams*, as a cornerstone of a novel form of theorizing—a basic yield of theoretical knowledge exactingly inferred from clinical findings regarding symptoms and dreams. Freud conceived the metapsychology—his basic psychoanalytic theory of mind—when he realized that these *conscious* experiences (symptoms and dreams) are governed by laws alien to consciousness itself. Further, these laws, although as rigorous and mechanistic as physical or physiological laws, are not physical; they are mental. To theorize this odd domain in which subjectivity merges with objective mechanism, a new metapsychological language had to be devised. In this regard, one might say that Freud realized two things about dreams: (1) the conscious, experiential essence of dreams is that they are hallucinated scenes; (2) their psychological essence is to have meaning and purpose—namely, the disguised fulfilment of unconscious wishes. This second thesis had epochal content and was announced in the first six chapters of *The Interpretation of Dreams*. But psychoanalysis as an unprecedented and singular mode of theoretical activity originated when it occurred to the theorist that these two theses—of conscious and unconscious—must in fact be intrinsically related. In particular, reasoned Freud, as dreams appear not only to signify, represent, or depict unconscious wishes, but to actually express and fulfil them, a dream, whatever it symbolizes, *must* occur as a lived experience.

The dream's narrative content alone provides the signifier to be deciphered by the clinical theorist of the dream book's first six chapters. But the dream itself, so to speak, cares most about something that exceeds interpretation. I am referring to the dream's existential status as something immediately lived through and experienced fully, placing it on equal footing with all conscious experience. Thus, there are two dimensions in dream formation that concur in the operation of the dream-work.

As the dream-work implements its primary process transformations to disguise conflicted ideas, it achieves simultaneously what is, according to Freud (1900a), "the most general and the most striking psychological characteristic of the process of dreaming: a thought, and as a rule a thought of something that is wished, is objectified in the dream, is represented as a scene, or, as it seems to us, is experienced" (p. 534). Or, in another formulation, "The dream wish . . . is hallucinated, and as hallucinated, meets with belief in the reality of its fulfilment . . . [and] counts as undisputed reality" (1917d, pp. 229, 234). Or: "Since a dream that shows a wish as fulfilled is believed during sleep, it does away with the wish and makes sleep possible" (1901a, p. 678). And with the express intention "to arrive at an understanding of [this hallucinatory activity] we . . . embark upon a discussion that will take us far afield" (1900a, p. 535). With these words, Freud opens the metapsychology of chapter 7 and thus inaugurates basic psychoanalytic theory as a whole.

The thesis of consciousness is that the dream is an hallucinatory experience. The thesis of the unconscious is that the dream fulfils a wish. In the proposition that founds psychoanalysis, these theses combine in the assertion of the unconscious determination of conscious experience—the revelation that unconscious desires are active in us and infuse our lived experience with hidden meaning and manifest intensity. This basic principle of connection of unconscious and conscious entails the formulation of one particular concept. This unique conception, binding theory to experience, is the concept of hallucinatory wish-fulfilment.

Freud wrote to Fliess on 3 January 1899: "It is dawning . . . that the key to hysteria really lies in dreams" (1950 [1892–1899], p. 276). And one month later: "Reality–wish-fulfilment: it is from this contrasting pair that our mental life springs" (p. 278). The origin of psychoanalysis in the study of dreaming created a circumstance wherein the historical priority of a scientific idea—that of hallucinatory wish-fulfilment—indicated a conceptual priority as well. From both these standpoints, the first assertion of basic psychoanalytic theory is: satisfaction can be hallucinated. I hope to show that the discovery of hallucinated satisfaction is in fact integral to the discovery of the dynamic unconscious. Together, these concepts afford the first sighting of the entire domain of psychic reality.

To provide the reader with a feel for this reality, I will first attempt a phenomenological analysis of hallucinated satisfaction. In what we are about to consider, the mind, through purely internal operations, generates an experienced reality. In Freud's classic accounts (1950 [1895], pp. 317–319; 1900a, pp. 565–567), a wishful impulse initiates a chain of events in the mind, which seeks out a memory of satisfaction. Once activated, this memory becomes present to conscious awareness. If we position ourselves as outside observers, we can say that this memory refers to an object from the past, one not now perceptually present. We know that even though a memory is present, an object is not. We can distinguish memory from perception, but the nascent subject under study cannot.

Let us now place ourselves in this subject's shoes. A memory becomes present to consciousness. Something is affirmed to be present. This presentation cannot possess any pre-given, intrinsic quality that could function as an index, "in the past". Any such apprehension is a complex judgement—a controlled blending of affirmation and negation that constitutes the function of reality testing (Freud, 1925h). To begin with, therefore, this affirmation of the presence of a memory is phenomenologically identical to an affirmation of the object which that memory intends. This absent object comes into view along with the memory. This is the key point: with the activation of memory, an object is seemingly present, and seeming presence is in truth a form of presence. There is no getting behind this condition without falling into an infinite regress of the sort, "It doesn't really seem present; it just seems to seem present".

A principle of subjectivity is therefore operative in the groundwork of wishing. Accordingly, writes Freud (1925h), "Originally the mere existence of a presentation was a guarantee of the reality of what was presented. The antithesis of subjective and objective does not exist from the first" (Freud, 1925h, p. 237). Now, by stepping back to the outside, we can see how, mediated by memory, this wishful affirmation of an absent object is the prototype for hallucination. Moreover, a wished-for object thus affirmed to be present has been consciously re-found in empirical reality. The wish is fulfilled.

In my discussion of the historical and conceptual priority of hallucinatory wish-fulfilment, a third species of priority has slipped in: that of ontogenesis, the development of the individual. I have tried to elucidate the Freudian hypothesis, inferred from dreams, that hallucinatory wish-fulfilment occurs in earliest mental life as a structural necessity. "Dreams ... have merely preserved for us ... a sample of the psychical apparatus's primary method of working. ... Dreaming is a piece of infantile mental life that has been superseded" (1900a, p. 567). It is perhaps immediately apparent that this postulation of hallucinated satisfaction must present formidable, if not insurmountable, difficulties for observational research into the foundations of basic psychoanalytic theory. I have tried to show how a principle of consciousness lies at the core of the theory—that for a psychoanalytic wish the belief in satisfaction is satisfaction itself. If we restrict ourselves to the outside position—the vantage point of standard science—we confront the limitative principle regulating any probing of subjectivity that would render it completely in objective terms (Bohr, 1932; Nagel, 1974). Brain science may explain blindness but not sight. This intractable elusiveness to experimental objectification is, I think, a matter that demands urgent clarification in light of the overreadiness with which some psychoanalysts have accepted proclamations refuting basic psychoanalytic theory. Such proclamations often emerge from infant observation research. Consider, for instance, the paradigmatic and influential work of Daniel Stern. Stern's claim, widely embraced, is that such fundamental concepts as infantile drive, hallucination, and fantasy, which were originally inferred from the psychoanalytic study of adults, are now disproved by sophisticated laboratory observation of infants themselves. But students of psychoanalytic theory should be as alert as Stern is himself to a methodological principle inherent to a theory of experience. As Stern (1985) carefully notes, "Developmental psychology can inquire about the infant only as the infant is observed. To relate observed behaviour to subjective experience, one must make inferential leaps. ... At best, the observations of an infant's available capacities can only help define the limits of subjective experience" (pp. 13–14; see also Merikle & Joordens, 1996). My aim here is not to present a critical account of Stern's theory (for this, see Opatow, 1989). Rather, it is to stress that when Stern cites the necessity for inferential leaps in a theory of experience, he is acknowledging that even his proximal observations take him only so near, and must be extended by concepts that cross the gap to subjectivity. These bridging concepts come from outside the field of observation—deriving, for Stern, from presuppositions regarding the nature of the self. Thus, no matter how rigorous and elegant the observational set-up producing his behavioural data, Stern's conclusions about infant experience—and, most saliently, infant hallucinations—are as ultimately dependent on speculative reconstruction as were Freud's. Nevertheless, the empiricist assumptions that mediate Stern's conjectures have almost entirely escaped scrutiny in his reception by an analytic community seeking solid observational ground.

If psychoanalysis is to adhere to its most radical calling as a theory of the determinants of conscious experience, there will always be a need in its theorizing for concepts that accomplish inferential leaps between the domains of outer appearance and inner experience. But our clinical science has amply demonstrated that we human beings abhor gaps of all kinds. Hence, in our theoretical activity we may seek objective ground as something more to cling to than to leap from. An inquiry into hallucinatory wish-fulfilment lays bare the severe antinomy in any attempt to objectify and observe the mind *in vivo*. It seems to me that in psychoanalysis the impulse to deny hallucination to the infant—rationalized on observational grounds—manifests the strenuous difficulty in perpetually enduring the conceptual strain at the core of a radical theory. Moreover, according to a correlation that I will develop further, the refutation of infant hallucination entails a concomitant rejection of unconscious fantasy and thus, in effect, of infantile sexuality.

So far I have concentrated on discussing the significance of hallucinatory wish-fulfilment in its historical priority both with regard to the origin of psychoanalysis itself and within its account of the individual's ontogenesis. Now I will focus on the conceptual priority of hallucinatory wish-fulfilment in the psychoanalytic theory of the mind. My major thesis is that the psychic reality of the dynamic unconscious is continuously grounded in the subjective reality of hallucinated satisfaction.

In a note at the close of chapter 6 of *The Interpretation of Dreams*, Freud (1900a) writes, "At bottom, dreams are nothing other than a particular *form* of thinking. . . . It is the *dream-work* which creates that form, and it alone is the essence of dreaming" (pp. 506–507). Thus, the truest significance of dreaming is surprisingly deemed to be not its unconscious motivation but, rather, its mode of activity—the primary process, the dream-work *per se*. This accords with

Rapaport's assertion (1960) that Freud's deepest concepts of the repressed unconscious and of intrapsychic conflict concern the hierarchical inhibition of lower by higher modes of mental activity, as well as the dynamic interaction of these antithetical modes. I mentioned earlier that it was this shift in emphasis, from what dreams mean to how they work, that inspired the seventh chapter and the commencement of basic psychoanalytic theory.

In the remainder of this section I turn to a study of unconscious fantasy—a clinical notion second to none and aimed at by every psychoanalytic intervention—as a means of bringing out the full theoretical significance of hallucinatory wish-fulfilment. I want in particular to explore the *efficacy* of unconscious fantasy—meaning its agency, its power to express and gratify unconscious wishes amid the material of ordinary adult experience. To this end I will focus on the notion, from Freud's chapter 7, of the need of the unconscious for transference, my interest in which was further stimulated by the eminent papers on transference by Loewald (1960), Arlow (1969), and Bird (1972). Loewald writes, "Without such transference of the intensity of the unconscious, of the infantile ways of experiencing life to present-day life and contemporary objects, human life becomes sterile and an empty shell" (1960, p. 250).

First I want to correlate and deepen the link between two principal aspects of transference: (1) as helping constitute the full meaning of *conscious* experience; (2) as realizing *unconscious* fantasies experientially, thus fulfilling unconscious desires. My question is this: How can an unconscious fantasy, by contributing elements to manifest conscious experience, be effectively actualized in its entirety?

Early in chapter 7, Freud offers this paradigmatic account of the relation of the dream's manifest and latent content:

> On this view a dream might be described as a *substitute for an infantile scene modified by being transferred on to a recent experience.* The infantile scene is unable to bring about its own revival and has to be content with returning as a dream. [Freud, 1900a, p. 546]

An unconscious wish strives to actualize a scene—to revive it as a conscious event. Whether that event is perceptual or hallucinatory is at root a matter of indifference, so long as the scene is reproduced in consciousness and has immediate experiential reality. This reminds us again that psychoanalysis is a theory of conscious experience, and that an unconscious wish achieves expression primarily in its impact on consciousness. What is asserted in chapter 7's theory of transference is that with the development of a structured mind, this impact can no longer be direct. Transference mediates the expression of the unconscious and transmits its impulsivity indirectly, as some effect on—or, rather, constituent of—conscious experience. This effect, no matter how remote, is the fulfilment of an unconscious desire. Recall again the idea that dreams must be hallucinations so that represented scenes are lived through and "meet with full belief". In little Anna's dream, the strawberries are there to be enjoyed. Only an affirmation—a "yes"—can fulfil a wish. This suggests that the conscious event expressing an unconscious wish must consist of more than a mere sensation or idea. It must be a felt affirmation, an assertion that something is true of, is a real part of, the actual world. Here is the thesis I will try to develop: what is transferred from unconscious to conscious in the movement up the ordered hierarchy of mind is *affirmation per se.*

First some general considerations. Psychoanalytic theory is simultaneously an objective model of the mind and an account of subjective experience. The theory comprises an uneasy coexistence of abstract and experiential terms. Hallucinatory wish-fulfilment refers concomitantly to a metapsychological process and (as is shown by dreams) to subjective experience. At the theoretical outset, metapsychology and phenomenology virtually coincide. As the mental apparatus matures, however, these two dimensions diverge while overlapping continuously. Thus, even while positing mental structure as a hierarchy of drive–defence conflicts, psychoanalysis remains a theory of experience. This is evident, for instance, in Brenner's formulation in *The Mind in Conflict* (1982): "As analysis progresses the drive-derivatives are less disguised, less distorted, and can be gratified with pleasure to an increasing degree" (p. 82). A correlation is posited between (1) the degree to which an unconscious wish can achieve manifest expression in consciousness and (2) its attendant fulfilment. Indeed, a drive can fulfil itself only insofar as it can prolong itself—can, as it were, "derivative" itself—into consciousness. This drive extension from latency to manifestation is the function of transference. In the conflictual dynamics underlying compromise formation, insufficient disguise leads to conscious unpleasure, which defences then function to prevent. All this is standard conflict theory.

What is less standard is the principle, both metapsychological and phenomenological, that the mechanism of unconscious wishes entails the mutual dependence of conscious and unconscious (see Freud, 1900a, pp. 562–564). The unconscious gains fulfilment predominantly as something conscious. Our minds function as an apparatus to achieve optimal gratification of unconscious fantasies—that is, their continuous actualization in consciousness as dreams, symptoms, traits, daydreams, enactments, masturbation fantasies, and the like. But, as we know, in all of this experience, the unconscious is expressed only by being disguised. What is it, we may ask, that passes through this sieve from unconscious to conscious and thus permits the unconscious to insert itself into consciousness? I will try to go further.

Let us consider again the transference leading to compromise formation in consciousness. When we clinically examine the drives and defences underlying compromise formation, we are bound to emphasize how conflicting intentions lead to distorted contents entering conscious awareness. I want to supplement this clinical focus with a metapsychological one. Recall the proposition, mentioned earlier, that the psychoanalytic theory of repression is grounded in the contemporary organismic principle of the hierarchical advance of structure. The deepest meaning of conflict pertains to an inhibitory boundary separating two modes of operation in the mental apparatus. This implies that in addition to combining antithetical mental *contents*, compromise formation must also refer to a functional concurrence of the two *modes*—the primary and secondary processes—in a unitary mental activity. This means that as the secondary process comes to overlay and inhibit primary process functioning (thus establishing the dynamic unconscious), the mechanism of wishes is hierarchically structuralized in the following way. In the primary process, the dream's hallucinated "other scene" ceases to function explicitly and independently and becomes instead a superimposed constituent of waking life. This requires that the primary process's sole purpose—to complete itself in hallucinated satisfaction—is intercepted and inhibited by the waking ego. In this sense, the ego's compromising or synthesizing activity works in two interrelated dimensions—dynamic and phenomenological. Operative in the first is the familiar dynamic need to express the unconscious to a degree that prevents primitive contents from reaching awareness. In the second is seen the phenomenological need (as it were) to express an hallucination—with that expression modified to a degree compatible with the ego's capacity for objective perception.

The latter compromise, devised by the ego between primary process hallucination and secondary process perception, points us to a further significance of the need of the unconscious for transference. With the dream scene rendered inoperative in waking life, some compromise between hallucination and perception becomes necessary if the unconscious is to achieve actual fulfilment as an experienced reality. This formal compromise that is reached by the ego between perception and hallucination, between the dream scene and the external world, yields a phenomenological *illusion.* The construction of this illusion pertains not only to the experiential mechanism of transference; it is integral to compromise formation in general. This illusion is the structurally modified continuation of a metapsychological hallucination. And a wishful hallucination is phenomenologically immanent in the illusory experience of transference.[1]

Moreover, it is important to note how this hallucinatory activity, when taken up by the ego, loses its phenomenal character and enters the deep structure of subjectivity—a domain formerly reserved in philosophy for Kant's transcendental ego. With the development of the ego, hallucination is subsumed, dropping away from the level of consciousness to the ego structure that generates experience.

---

[1]A comparison with Winnicott's (1964) famous notion of illusion would serve to clarify the subtle relation of Winnicott to Freud. This task cannot be done justice here. However, it may be noted that Winnicott (1) holds that the immanence of hallucination in ordinary experience allows a deep-lying sense that the world is our creation and, to that extent, subjectively matters; (2) recommends clinically that the ratio of transference components be watched for a shift towards objectivity and "usage".

As transference operates ubiquitously, the resulting illusions pervasively infiltrate conscious awareness. It follows that the efficacy of unconscious fantasies—their capacity to affect conscious experience and gain fulfilment in it—is dynamically grounded in the mind's capacity for hallucinatory wish-fulfilment. The psychic reality of unconscious fantasy has its abiding source in the subjective reality of hallucinated satisfaction. Beneath all unconscious fulfilments—be they enactments, symptoms, or traits—lies an abortive hallucination.

In this way, it is possible for the conscious affirmation of an illusory truth to effect the fulfilment of unconscious desire. The psychic reality of an unconscious wish, split from its hallucinatory source, regains experiential reality as a felt affirmation. Then the psychic reality of unconscious fantasy lies in its function as medium between hallucination and perception.

The importance of affirmation in this conception has been endorsed not only by Molly Bloom ("And yes I said yes I will Yes"—James Joyce, *Ulysses*). It is also supported by Brenner's formulation (1982) that every defence against a drive derivative must involve a kind of denial or negation (p. 76). Only an affirmation can be denied. And only an affirmation can fulfil a wish. The drive therefore emerges into compromise formation as an affirmation in consciousness. What transference sends forth from unconscious to conscious, from hallucination to perception, is affirmation *per se*.

I was surprised to find that this organic movement in mental life manifests an inner necessity that can, it would seem, be directly *intuited*. The following vignette illustrates the clinical import of this perspective on transference. I was teaching a course in analytic psychotherapy in a biologically oriented psychiatry program. The residents were a smart group who approached analytic theory with a combination of fascination and scepticism. I was presenting to them a patient who, during the termination phase of his treatment, had a recurrence of his obsessional symptom involving cars. The patient had largely resolved his painful feelings of being a lifelong mama's boy and nerd. The father was mostly out of the picture, except for one exhilarating childhood memory in which the patient was lifted high onto a rock by the father near the family's summer cabin. In early adolescence, living under his mother's protective gaze, the patient first developed an obsessional interest in cars, especially sports cars. He spent hours spotting cars on the street, reading auto magazines, and visiting dealers' showrooms. This symptom would wax and wane, and it vanished as he reached adulthood. As he expected termination to be like the painful leaving of a good father, the patient was surprised to be having no feelings about it at all. Instead, his obsession with cars returned. He could not get them out of his mind. They interfered with his work, kept him up at night, and drew him compulsively to haunt car showrooms in the evenings. But he could never find the right car.

PATIENT: I keep going to showrooms, but I'm always disappointed—and I've been feeling sad—because I'm leaving you? I saw these starving children on TV last night, and I began to cry.

THERAPIST: Those children are abandoned.

PATIENT: Yes—like me without a father.

THERAPIST: But you had him once—at the rock.

PATIENT: Yes—and I felt like a normal kid then—athletic and not a nerd. Then he disappeared, and it was like a different life.

THERAPIST: I think the car may be a souvenir from the first life.

PATIENT: Now I remember his car, a '55 Plymouth—the year I was born. He would drive to the rock—he was the best driver in the world—then he sold the car. It was when he lost his job, when JFK was shot—that's when he changed. He bought an older car, and I didn't like it as much. Then several months later I dreamed of the first car again, perfect and new. I still remember that dream.

THERAPIST: You still have it.

PATIENT [*begins to cry silently and weeps on and off for the rest of the session*].

I did not immediately disclose to the residents that the obsession with cars now disappeared again, but instead asked them what they thought happened to it. "It can't continue", said one. "No way", said another. "Impossible", said a third. These residents, as I mentioned, were not knowingly Freudian.

Desire and knowledge

A comparison of the psychoanalytic and psychological viewpoints brings out not only the unparalleled concept of hallucinatory wish-fulfilment and its exponent, unconscious fantasy, but also what is most distinctive about the psychoanalytic unconscious. Many cognitive experiments have conclusively demonstrated the existence of unconscious perception, consistent with psychoanalytic research on subliminal perception (Shevrin, 1992). These phenomena lead one to believe that the unconscious is a perceptual organ—an idea coherent with its conception as a form of repressed consciousness.

Most impressive in the cognitive research are conclusions pertaining to qualitative differences in important aspects of conscious and unconscious processing. Several cognitive studies point convergently to major organizational and systematic implications of the conscious/unconscious distinction (Merikle, 1992; Merikle & Joordens, 1996). Conscious awareness is accompanied by a heightening of organizational level and functional control, a correlation also shown by neuroscience (Libet, 1985). Consciousness is a prerequisite for the instigation of a predictive strategy (Merikle, 1992) and is integral to the binding of mental contents to specific contexts (Marcel, 1983). Consciousness is thus characterized by secondary process and binding, and the unconscious by unbinding and mobility. Consciousness is also necessary for the regulatory capacities of repudiation and negation, a cognitive finding echoed by neuroscience (Libet, 1985) and emphasized later here. Further, conscious influence overrides and controls unconscious factors when both are present (Merikle & Joordens, 1996). All of these propositions are in full accord with the hierarchical theory of mental structure in the topographical model of psychoanalysis (Freud, 1900a, 1915e).

However, it is of great note that the cognitive research project does not venture any theoretical explanation of these fundamental correlations in mental activity and functioning. Psychoanalysis suggests that this omission is linked to the framework of standard cognitive theory, which ties motivation to consciousness and therefore rejects any notion of unconscious intention (Shevrin et al., 1996). This theoretical position is then reflected in a prevalent research methodology which, while revealing the correlations, effectively denies that all of the cognitive activities under study exist as aspects of motivational states. In this section I will stress the indispensability of this motivational condition in the psychoanalytic theory of cognition.

Freud (1915c) regarded the mind as an apparatus in order to root its organismic function in a capacity to do the work of gratifying instinctual demands, "the demands made upon the mind for work in virtue of its connection with the body" (p. 122). For psychoanalysis, reality is most basically the reality of the body and of physical need. Thus, asserts Freud in the Project (1950 [1895]), unpleasure is our sole means of education (p. 370). Moreover, mental process is initiated predominantly by wishes, and cognition occurs in the mind's movement from felt need to experienced satisfaction. All thinking, states Freud (1900a), is a substitute for an hallucinatory wish and occurs within the tension arc of unfulfilled desires (pp. 567, 602).

If the mind's prime function is to cope with physical need, its mode of action must be determined in accordance with this genesis and purpose. The mind first generates a wish expressible in intentional form and then proceeds to fulfil it. The joint conceptions of a mental apparatus operating to satisfy wishes, and of thought as a substitute for hallucinated satisfaction, indicate a deep dichotomy in thought itself. Because there can be effective hallucinatory fulfilment of certain wishes, primarily sexual, the mental apparatus can avail itself of two fundamentally different modes of processing these wishes. If all thought is inscribed in a wish, then cognition is profoundly conditioned by the apparatus's mode of wish-fulfilment—by whether its mental operations point to an objective reality in the external world or to that of an hallucinated scene. Modes of cognition necessarily follow from the definition of reality. The clinical discovery of hallucinated satisfaction reveals a novel realm of empirical consciousness called psychic reality, which in turn entails a whole new domain of cognitive psychology. Cognition, as our principal means of apprehending reality, must resonate with the structural principles of the reality it would grasp.

Psychoanalysis identifies a mode of mental functioning that presses towards the hallucinated presentation of the objects of desire. This thought activity, as unpreventable as it is nonveridical, is at odds with any adaptive relation to the external world. It is only because this hallucinated satisfaction breaks down in the case of vital needs, such as hunger, that the apparatus is driven by unpleasure to inhibit this activity and, hence, opens out to another scene of action and awareness—the external world we have in common. Therefore, I want to stress that, in contrast to the standard cognitive conception (Merikle, 1992), the psychoanalytic unconscious is not most deeply formulated as a preparatory forestage in the attainment of empirical consciousness. Rather, *the psychoanalytic unconscious is, to begin with, an original mode of consciousness itself.* This is why, as Freud (1915e) often emphasized, the unconscious bears all the attributes of conscious entities, excepting awareness. As clinically seen, the unconscious corresponds to this inhibited dynamic thrust towards hallucinatory consciousness. The unconscious is at root a repressed consciousness. The relation of the unconscious and consciousness is therefore best seen as constitutive rather than causal. The unconscious *constitutes* conscious experience even as it perturbs it. Consciousness harbours a dimension of mental depth and is constituted by mental activities that are not themselves conscious. The psychoanalytic unconscious is specifically mental and furnishes, as it were, a substructure for consciousness. These ideas are elaborated below.

One can see further how the unconscious originates in the repression of consciousness by considering that the inhibition of hallucinatory consciousness is first motivated by the felt pain of an intensifying need (hunger). The reality principle, which compels rejection of the failed hallucination, is therefore only a modification, a refinement, of the pleasure principle. For reality registers first as pain. The dynamic unconscious thus originates in psychic pain—in a wounding of consciousness.[2]

The clinical study of dreams and symptoms revealed, of course, that this inhibited, repressed mode of mental activity is perpetually active even as its path to hallucinatory immediacy is blocked.

---

[2] Here my exposition diverges from Freud's notion of an original unrepressed domain of unconscious mentation. Previously I tried to show, in agreement with Schur, that the psychogenesis of both ego and id occurs in the cleavage of a primal wish (Opatow, 1993).

The clue to its nature is once again the need of the unconscious for transference. The unconscious still achieves expression—that is, perceptual actualization in consciousness—but now only in modified form. This mediation, whose executive agency is the ego, allows unconscious fulfilments to interpenetrate empirical consciousness and to coexist with, and contribute to, an adaptive relation to the external world. This, as I have argued above, is the true essence of compromise formation.

In the developmental theory of psychoanalysis, the infant's transition from hallucinated satisfaction to the breast in the external world not only implies a particular object—it marks an advance in objectivity itself. This is borne out by the recent discovery in early infancy of cross-modal perception—the combining of sense predicates in the conception of a unitary object (Stern, 1985, pp. 47–51). But this advance in objectivity points to one in subjectivity as well. The repression of hallucinatory activity at once founds the dynamic unconscious and inaugurates a structured ego consciousness of the external world. This interdependency of subjective structure and object world provides a supreme principle of mental development. In this regard, Ferenczi states, "The development of the reality sense is represented by a succession of repressions, to which mankind was compelled, not through a spontaneous 'striving toward development', but through necessity, . . . a demanded renunciation" (1913, p. 236). Repression, then, is constitutive for the human subject. Rather than being a preliminary activity that *causes* a conscious event, the unconscious helps *constitute* the inner structure of experiencing consciousness. Each increase in external objectivity reflects an intensification of subjective inwardness and inner structure. The unconscious, in this sense, is Freud's answer to Kant's transcendental ego.

This hypothesis has a further crucial significance. In psychoanalysis, the object world is first and foremost generated in the experience of desire. This was already apparent in the motivated transition from hallucinatory to external objects. Psychoanalysis gives priority to the development of the object of need (and of want) as the prototype for all objects as intended in perception and knowledge. In the extrapolations of Freud, ranging from Melanie Klein to René Spitz, even the purest cognition of external objects rests on a fantasy substrate of incorporative desire. By stressing this fundamental character of human desire, psychoanalysis achieves a unification of diverse theories of consciousness and thought that have arisen in the history of philosophy.[3] And it connects a theory of existence with a theory of treatment.

I now turn to some distinctive implications for the theory of thinking. In psychoanalysis, thought refers not only to formal operations on representational elements. It is more than information processing, for it proceeds in the unfolding of a wish. It is a way of reaching an object. Both the primary and the secondary processes refer not only to representational transformations in thought, they also supply thought with representational content—the object we think about. This always pertains ultimately to an object of desire, be it one of raw need or of curiosity and research. That the unconscious abides repressed in consciousness means that some primitive object always lies embedded within the official objects of our cognitive interest. By virtue of this source of objectivity in desire, we are allowed to live intimately *with* the things of the world rather than merely beside them.

Ferenczi underscores how the sense of reality is formed through successive repressions and demanded renunciations. In this developmental progression, each early phase of repression, whether targeting sexual wishes to devour or sadistic wishes to dominate and control, further increases the experienced objectivity of objects and their degree of otherness. Furthermore, Freud describes how real love—as love for another—is undercut by these primitive oral and anal impulses that seek to abolish the separateness of objects (1915c, pp. 138–139). Repression, it would seem,

---

[3] Psychoanalysis establishes a theoretical ground of connection of conscious and unconscious, unlike the conceptual dissonance afflicting, say, a theory of phenomenology and synapses. It was Freud's teacher, Brentano, who laid down the lasting principle that consciousness, and mental life in general, is characterized by an essential attribute of intrinsic intentionality—the object-directedness ("aboutness") of the mental, what Russell called "propositional attitudes" (Searle, 1983). Moreover, ever since Kant, and especially Husserl, we know that the structure of the object world is intrinsically determined by the structure of conscious subjectivity. Thus, for Kant (1781), the categories that integrate objective experience reflect forms of inner synthesis occurring in consciousness. Subjectivity and objectivity are hence strongly interconnected and develop in tandem, both in these theories of mind and in psychoanalysis.

first conditions our capacity to love before disturbing it. As it engenders the dynamic unconscious, repression supplies inner structure to an empirical consciousness that can think and love. This is what it means to say that repression is constitutive for the human subject.

It is important here to note that these structuring acts of mind correspond to what Freud called "primal repressions". What is being subjected to repression is not just a particular instance (as in a clinical moment) of some wishful impulse or object relation, but rather a whole category or modality of objectivity and desire. Thus, what is at stake is not only what is no longer experienced, but what becomes newly available to experience.[4]

To see further how primal repression mediates the interrelation of subjective structure and external world, one must return to the prototype of this whole relation—the repression that bears on hallucinatory wish-fulfilment. If we consider that wishful hallucination must be repressed as a precondition for any stable relation to, and testing of, external reality—a capacity forfeit in dreams—we understand that this repression does not recur anew, one hallucination at a time. Instead, it is a structured inhibition of the entire hallucinatory thrust of the primary processing of wishes. Hallucination as a mode of operation of the mental apparatus, impeded from direct expression, is modified to contribute to objective perception. This repudiation of an entire mode of wish-fulfilment—not just of a particular hallucination, but of hallucinatory activity *per se*—is just what is meant by primal repression. Such repression is therefore as much developmental as it is defensive.

An hallucinatory presentation, thus repressed, is stripped of the immediacy of perceptual presence and may become instead a memory, and explicitly so—an object phenomenologically "in the past", absent and lost (Opatow, 1988, 1989). As Freud notes,

> The antithesis of subjective and objective does not exist from the first. It only comes into being from the fact that thinking

---

[4] These primal repressions are not identical with the defences encountered in ordinary clinical work, but are a precondition for them all. For an extended discussion of this primal repression and its relation to identification and the development of sexuality and the ego, see Opatow (1993).

> has the capacity to bring before the mind once more something that has once been perceived, by reproducing it as a presentation without that external object still having to be there. The first and immediate aim, therefore, of reality-testing is not to *find* an object in real perception . . . but to *refind* [it]. . . . But it is evident that a precondition for this reality-testing is that objects shall have been lost which once brought real satisfaction. [Freud, 1925h, pp. 237–238]

If one examines in this light the conceptual structure of the psychoanalytic unconscious, it becomes apparent that its distinction with respect to other notions of the unconscious has importantly to do with the extraordinary significance of negation. In the standard empirical sciences, especially those grounded in mathematics, negation is a logical operator for the cancelling and total erasure of its term. For instance, the prevailing view in cognitive science takes the computer as a fundamental metaphor for human mental processes (Shevrin et al., 1996). In this computational model, consider the information-processing sequence *p or q; q* is not *p* and replaces it. The two symbols represent differences; if an element is *p*, it is not *q*, says the law of identity. This is how logical negation is typically employed. But the psychoanalytic concept of negation, the *un* in the unconscious, is different. I think that its sense is conveyed, with incomparable aptness, in the Devil's declaration to Ivan Karamazov:

> By some pretemporal assignment, which I have never been able to figure out, I am appointed "to negate". . . . [Affirmation] alone is not enough for life. . . . So they made me negate and life came about. . . . They say "live", because without you there would be nothing, nothing would ever happen, there would be no events. [People] suffer of course, but they still live, they live really, not in fantasy. [Dostoevsky, 1880, p. 642]

Returning once more to the hungry baby and the psychoanalytic effort to theorize experience, consider that the very first encounter with negation, both experientially and theoretically, occurs as a lived experience of *pain*—the pain of increasing need tension. This pain—like a toothache, simultaneously mental and physical—marks a direct point of body–mind interaction. The one way for the mind to become active in response to this pain—a primary experience of being helplessly overwhelmed, of pure passivity—is to institute a negation. This act of negation is not something abstract or syntactical; it pertains to the negativity of consciousness.[5] Cognition properly (that is, symbolically) begins when this pain of instinctual need becomes experienced as *lack*, a negation that constitutes the wish—an awareness that something could be absent. Conceptual negation is what the mind does with instinctual pain. An experiential nothingness lies at the source of cognitive negation. The failed hallucination, once repressed, is convertible to a *representation*—something standing for an absence—and hence becomes available for symbolic processing. We note a hierarchy of negations: affective repudiation prompts the repression of the unconscious, which is continually operative in the logical negations in consciousness. Thus does early repression pound hallucination into thought. Accordingly, recent studies in infant cognition, contrary to Piaget, find incipient symbolic capacities in the first weeks of life (Mandler, 1990; Spelke, 1988).

But all thinking must require negation. By thought I mean not the rote working out of algorithms occurring in, say, present-day computers or the DNA transcription of proteins. On this operational level, the rule is always given in advance, without having to be in any way understood (Searle, 1980). Few would hold that this merits the name of thought. I am referring instead to something computers have not yet achieved and, according to some theorists, never will: the capacity to set goals, to anticipate, and, most important, to reflect on its activity and modify its strategy for attaining its goal (Changeux & Connes, 1995). This, so to speak, would mean rejecting its hallucinations. It is this critical ability to reflect and take distance from itself—a capacity that may depend on pain—that implicates negation in true operational intelligence. Thus, again: all thinking requires negation. And this negativity is rooted in the desire of a living being. Desire, then, is implicitly a concep-

[5] This is the negation inherent to the act of reflection by which consciousness takes distance from the immediacy of experience to become "aware of awareness". For a cognate concept of consciousness, see Freud (1900a, p. 616); for an extended discussion of the ideas in the above paragraph, see Opatow (1989).

tual apparatus. Psychoanalysis, by grounding thought in life, thus postulates the inseparability of knowledge and desire.

The repression of the primary process, in aborting and subsuming its hallucinatory aim, helps to constitute a higher stage of mental organization—now including an idea of desired objects in the world. From this we can state that the divisions of the world into internal and external, and of the mind into conscious and unconscious, reflects a structural concomitance. Moreover, this repression of primary process is not merely that of a particular mental content but of an entire modality of mental functioning. In psychoanalysis, the *un* in the unconscious means not so much *not* conscious as *under* conscious.

And what mentality is under consciousness?—a structural base that will not stay still; a striving towards hallucination dynamically intercepted and infused into the flow of awareness, penetrating and interweaving with consciousness to be partially realized in the external world. We call such an impulse, which seeks to restore primitive contents and operations to perceptual experience, an unconscious wish.

Let me return to the idea that the two separate categories of *reality*, the material and the psychic, rooted, respectively, in external perception and hallucinatory belief, demand two kinds of thinking to apprehend them. This duality of thought corresponds, of course, to the primary and secondary processes. Thinking is, hence, defined by its divergent end points or objectives—for Freud (1900a), "perceptual identity" and "thought identity" (p. 602). How does such a differential objectivity determine these distinctive modes of thought? Thinking, in general, refers to a succession of mental contents ordered by a set of logical rules. For instance, the rationality that characterizes the secondary process presumably exemplifies the laws of identity, excluded middle, and contradiction—the so-called laws of thought. Experience shows that implementing these procedures reliably establishes the reappearance of a desired object in the external world (while helping to avoid unpleasant surprises). The conceptual organization of the mind permits the structure of the external world to be internally represented as determinations of thought. Freud (1900a) stresses that for this to occur, the elements of thought must be appreciated and handled solely on the basis of their conceptual significance; they must be totally abstracted from their attendant affects of pleasure and pain (p. 602). Able to achieve this only partially, we all fall victim to wishful thinking. If the secondary process would bracket all affectivity in thought, the primary process, conversely, suspends logical meanings while moving us towards pleasure—ultimately, the pleasure of hallucinated satisfaction. Here ideational elements become reduced to mere conduits of affective intensity. I want to examine this more closely.

Logic designates the ordering of propositions in thought, with each proposition comprising a subject and a predicate: "Socrates is a man." As forms of thought, both the primary and the secondary processes necessarily operate on these ideational elements. In the case of the secondary process, we can state straight away that the sequence of ideas is governed mainly by the standard rules of logical implication.

But what of the syntax of the primary process? Consider an element in the movement of a thought, and hence also of a wish. The inferential processes that generate meaning occur only as expressions of motivational force. It is as if, fought over by the primary and secondary processes, thinking must decide at every moment whether its very next element will be determined more by logic or by pleasure.

At every point of its trajectory, thinking therefore moves along two gradients. These gradients specify tendencies in the propagation of thought that are so deeply incommensurable as to exist in virtually orthogonal dimensions. In his great study of Freud, Ricoeur stresses that psychoanalysis is uniquely mandated to comprise theoretically an irreducible antinomy of force and meaning for an account of subjectivity: "It is easier to fall back on a disjunction: either an explanation in terms of energy, or an understanding in terms of phenomenology. It must be recognized, however, that Freudianism exists only on the basis of its refusal of this disjunction" (Ricoeur, 1970, p. 66). Moreover, this essential duality in the theory stems from the substance of its main subject: "That which is represented in affects and which does not pass into ideas is desire qua desire" (p. 453). In psychoanalysis, the representational elements of thought are carriers simultaneously of semantic meaning and instinctual force. This elemental conflict of force and meaning, or, one could say, of instinctual force and implicative force, acts like a torsion that can effectively shear apart the propositional structures of wishes, ripping the predicates from subjects. A similar, and related, predicament was noted by T. S. Eliot (1943) in his attempt to give timelessness linguistic form when he wrote of words straining, cracking, and sometimes breaking under the burden; under the tension, slipping, sliding, and perishing (Eliot, 1943, p. 19). For Freud, the conceptual order gives way under instinctual strain—as unbound predicates, or object attributes, coalesce on a path, a syntactical highway to the inner object of desire. Thus, the syntax of the primary process, or of instinctual force in general, resorts to—perhaps creates—the paleological form known as *predicative identification.* Here force overwhelms meaning, and identity overrides difference. An affective insistence makes use of common predicates so as to force the equivalence of objects. Hence, all finding is a re-finding. A syntax is thus provided for primary process transformations.[6]

If we now think back to the earlier account of transference as comprising both cognition and phenomenology in a single sweep, we are prepared to expect that the movement of *thought* in predicative identification is integral to the means of assembly of the *perceptual* illusions of transference. This means that, in the expression of an unconscious wish, the semantic and syntactic aspects of the primary process are internally related. (In contrast, for standard cognitive theory, the relation of semantics and syntax stems from basically separate levels of cognitive structure—see Pylyshyn, 1989). I want to explore this connection in the primary process between the paralogic it applies and the hallucinatory truth it asserts. Consider that an unconscious wish, even if rooted in syncretic memories, expresses an intention. It exists as a differentiated structure of subject, act, and object and hence is represented in propositional form. But no piece of syntax creates the drive that invests it. Rather, the drive inhabits the form and can be lifted off it

[6] In this paralogical reasoning, different objects with any predicates or adjectives in common are equated in their entirety. First discovered in schizophrenia research as the principal means by which delusional ideas are generated from affective needs (von Domarus, 1944), it is also variously manifest in the dream-work.

or compressed into any part of it. In the primary processing of an unconscious wish, its full intensity can be condensed into any of the constituent elements of the wish's propositional structure.

Now, consider again that in waking life the hallucinatory thrust of the primary process—the dream's "other scene"—is reduced to a structural factor superimposed on the given perceptual reality. The impulse seeks to actualize, to manifest—to imprint—its scene on consciousness. The two scenes—unconscious and conscious, or fantasy and real—are aligned and matched in the ego so as to bring them into optimal coincidence. The more characteristics they have in common and the more global their significance, the more reactive the configuration. Now, unconscious fantasy, tasting the blood of consciousness, mobilizes its drive intensity and releases it towards these common elements. With this convergence onto joint predicates, the drive is concentrated in the intersection of fantasy and real. The unconscious impulse, riding its predicate-bridge, can now cross over and emerge into consciousness as an attribute of experience.

In this way—at unconsciously selected elements of consciousness—infusions of intensity are emitted into awareness and hence, *in situ*, constitute experienced affects. These fresh affects, unconsciously derived and of alien descent, impart dissonant new valuations that disturb the prior integration of experience. These insurgent, disruptive affects must be made to cohere in experience. To span and resolve them in a new synthesis requires, however, a reinterpretation of the entire perceptual scene. Hence there evolves a restabilized but altered perception, which, pushed forth as truth, forms the manifest content of the transference illusion. Thus do unconscious impulses attain experiential reality and enter the life-world as affective illusions.

I have attempted to show here how the conscious affirmation of an illusory truth achieves the fulfilment of unconscious desire. More generally, I have tried to set forth the psychoanalytic unconscious as a unique structure of human consciousness.

CHAPTER TWO

What is affect?

Mark Solms

Affect has both psychic and physical manifestations

It has been obvious since ancient times—to anyone who cared to look—that affect can be influenced directly, and in specific ways, by physical and chemical means. In the historical epoch during which psychoanalysis was born, the most prominent examples of such influences were (1) neurosyphilitic infection and (2) alcohol, morphine, and cocaine intoxication. As a neurological clinician and researcher, Freud was thoroughly familiar with these topics. He was also aware of the addictive (that is to say, motivational) properties of alcohol, morphine, and cocaine. This knowledge no doubt contributed to the theory of affect that he later developed.

This chapter was first published in German—under the title "Was sind Affekte?"—in *Psyche, 50* (1996): 485–522. Earlier versions were presented at the Fifth IPA Conference on Psychoanalytic Research, "Advances in Our Understanding of Affects: Clinical Implications" (10 March 1995) and at a meeting of the Neuro-Psychoanalysis Center of the New York Psychoanalytic Institute (3 June 1995).

According to Freud's classical affect theory, all behaviour is ultimately motivated by the pursuit of pleasure and the avoidance of unpleasure, but pleasurable and unpleasurable emotions are merely conscious manifestations of an underlying quasi-physiological process. Freud formulated this underlying process in terms of his concept of "drive" [*Trieb*], which he defined as:

> a concept on the frontier between the mental and the somatic, as the psychical representative of the stimuli originating from within the organism and reaching the mind, as a measure of the demand made upon the mind for work in consequence of its connection with the body. [Freud, 1915c, pp. 121–122]

This suggests that, in Freud's classical formulation, physical and chemical influences upon our emotions could be understood as conscious manifestations of the influence that they exert upon the drives. However, it is precisely this connection between affect theory and drive theory that has brought Freud's conceptualization of emotion into disrepute among many modern analysts, who see no place for quasi-physiological concepts in a science of the mind. Various purely psychological theories that reverse the dependent relationship between emotions and drives (now conceptualized as "motivations") and replace the concept of drive with a purely representational conception of affect have since been advanced (e.g. Brenner, 1976; Dahl, 1979; Emde, 1988; Kernberg, 1988, 1992; Lichtenberg, 1988, 1989; Sandler, 1972; Schwartz, 1988). However, these alternative theories do not begin to explain the undeniable fact that emotions can be influenced directly by physical and chemical means.

This important connection between affect and physiology is disregarded, notwithstanding the fact that modern analysts also have to take account of the reality that *various pharmacological agents are now commonly used in the treatment of emotional disorders*. It is noteworthy in this respect that it is precisely in relation to the *affective* symptoms of mental illness (i.e. the very symptoms that Freud attempted to explain in quasi-physiological terms)[1] that psy-

[1] Freud is sometimes regarded as one of the founders of psychopharmacology, in that he recommended cocaine as a treatment for melancholia and other mental disorders (Freud, 1884e, 1885f). Freud also anticipated the subsequent

chopharmacology has achieved its greatest successes.[2] Whatever our views may be of the therapeutic value of these agents in relation to the underlying mental illnesses that they aim to treat, the fact remains that they do directly alter the emotional state of the patient. And since we use our psychoanalytical theories to explain and treat the identical clinical phenomena, we have a compelling reason to reconcile our conceptualizations of affect with the relevant physiological facts.

Any satisfactory theory of affect also needs to take account of the fact that the basic emotions—in contrast to other classes of mental phenomena—are typically associated with conspicuous somatic symptoms. In the case of anxiety, for example, the characteristic feelings of unpleasure are frequently accompanied by palpitations, sweating, nausea, diarrhoea, faintness, dizziness, urinary frequency, muscular tension, tremor, chest pain, fatigue, choking sensations, shortness of breath, headache, paraesthesia, or sensory hyper-reactivity. These somatic symptoms, in turn, reflect underlying physiological changes, such as (in the case of anxiety) the re-direction of blood away from the skin and gut to the cardiac and voluntary musculature, an increase in respiratory rate, heart rate, and blood pressure, and a reduction in salivatory and mucous secretions. Freud attempted to explain these somatic correlates of emotion along evoutionary biological lines (Darwin, 1872), by suggesting that they were "reproductions of very early, perhaps even

---

developments in the field just mentioned. Consider for example, the following passage: "The future may teach us to exercise a direct influence, by means of particular chemical substances, on the amounts of energy and their distribution in the mental apparatus. It may be that there are still undreamt-of possibilities of therapy" (Freud, 1940a, p. 182).

[2] Monoamine oxidase inhibitors, tricyclics, and serotonin uptake blockers are effective antidepressants. They also prevent some forms of anxiety (panic attacks). These drugs act on the cholinergic, serotonergic, and noradrenergic systems of the brain and spinal cord. Lithium, the physiological action of which is unclear, is effective in terminating and preventing manic episodes and some forms of depression. The benzodiazepines control generalized forms of anxiety. These drugs enhance the (inhibitory) action of certain GABA receptors in the brain. The phenothiazines, butyrophenones, thioxanthenes, and dibenzodiazepines control the positive symptoms of schizophrenia. They are also effective in terminating some manic episodes. These drugs block the dopamine systems of the brain.

pre-individual, experiences of vital importance"—which should be regarded as "universal, typical and innate hysterical attacks, as compared to the recently and individually acquired attacks, which occur in hysterical neuroses and whose origin and significance as mnemic symbols have been revealed by analysis" (Freud, 1926d, p. 133). In other words, Freud considered the somatic manifestations of affect to be (inherited) adaptive reactions to the environmental situations in which the basic emotions originally occurred.[3] Whether or not we accept this formulation, here we have another definite connection between emotions and physiology, and this connection needs to be accommodated within our theories.

Despite these undeniable connections between affect and objective somatic phenomena, there is of course also something essentially subjective about affect. It is in the essence of an emotion that you *feel* it. In fact, there seems to be something especially subjective about affect. This is the reason why the topic of emotion was, until recently (Damasio, 1994, 1999; Panksepp, 1998), regarded with such suspicion by academic psychologists. How, these colleagues argued, is one to define and measure a variable that can never be perceived objectively? Here they came up against all of the methodological problems that have so bedevilled psychoanalytical researchers. As a result, the academic psychologists concentrated their efforts on the behavioural, somatic, and physiological manifestations of affect, which they all too often confused with the essence of affect itself. Psychoanalysts were quick to point out this error. However, are we not committing a similar error ourselves—at least in principle—when we neglect the physical aspects of affect and study only the subjective feelings?

We therefore face a fundamental question: *how can it be that affect is an essentially subjective state and yet is inextricably connected with the objective body?* Before we can begin to provide a psychoanalytical solution to this problem, we will need to address ourselves to a still broader question, namely, *where does one situate the physical body in a psychoanalytic theory of the mind?* This is the basic question that I would like to address in this chapter, in relation to the problem of affect. Exasperating as such questions are, I do not see

[3] Inherited reactions of this type have survival value. Biologists attribute them to "reflex" or "instinct" [*Instinkt*], depending upon their complexity.

how we can avoid them in psychoanalysis. In fact, I believe that the whole of psychoanalysis is predicated upon particular assumptions about the relationship between the mind and the body. I will now briefly outline these general assumptions (discussed in greater detail in Solms, 1997d), before I return to the specific problem of affect.

Reality is perceived in two different ways

Psychoanalytic research, like every other form of research, begins with the perceptual data of consciousness. Freud divided these data into two broad categories—namely, *physical* perceptions (of things that occur in the world around us) and *psychic* perceptions (of things that occur inside our own selves). He located these two classes of perception on the "two sensory surfaces" of consciousness (Freud, 1900a, p. 574), which he also described as the "two terminal points of our knowledge" (Freud, 1940a, pp. 144, 196). This classification of the contents of consciousness is neither especially controversial nor outdated; it coincides *roughly* with the conventional distinction between "non-reflexive" and "reflexive" consciousness (Marcel, 1988). It also coincides with Kant's distinction between "simple awareness" and "self-awareness" (cf. Brook, 1994). Bion (1970) based his influential conception of "reality sensual and psychic" upon precisely the same distinction.

Psychoanalysts study reality from the viewpoint of the *internal* surface of consciousness. Our scientific goal is to explain the phenomena that are registered on this surface, within a natural–causal framework. Accordingly, the object of psychoanalytic research is that aspect of reality which determines introspective consciousness. Freud's justification for describing this aspect of reality in *psychic* terms need not be repeated in detail here (Freud, 1915e, pp. 166–171; 1940b; pp. 282–286). His essential argument was that a psychic conception of the internal determinants of consciousness—even though they are themselves unconscious—"enabled psychology to take its place as a natural science like any other" (Freud, 1940a, p. 158). This inserted our private thoughts and feelings into a natural causal framework. On the basis of this argument, psychoanalysts describe the internal processes that lie below the threshold of consciousness as if they, too, were subjectively conscious states. This conception of the mind is the most fundamental premise of our science. (Physicists employ a similar conception when they describe non-sensory *physical* processes—such as the phenomena of ultrasound and infrared—as if they were extensions of our *external* senses. Like psychoanalysts, they thereby transform those processes into data that *can* be described in figurative, perceptual terms.) Insofar as psychoanalysis aims by this approach to provide a comprehensive account of the field of psychic processes, and "to establish the laws which they obey and to follow the mutual relations and interdependencies unbroken over long stretches" (Freud, 1940a, p. 159), it is a basic science of "psychical reality".

The term "psychical reality" refers to the unconscious reality within us, when it is considered from the viewpoint of subjective awareness. However, Freud always acknowledged that the reality within us can *also* be represented as a *physical* thing, via our *external* sensory perception, since "the mental apparatus . . . is also known to us in the form of an anatomical preparation" (Freud, 1900a, p. 536). Accordingly, the object of study of psychoanalysis can be described *either* as a mental experience (from the viewpoint of internal perception) *or* as a physical organ (from the viewpoint of external perception). Psychoanalysis describes it mentally; anatomy and physiology describe it physically.

One striking implication of this fundamental conceptualization of the relationship between mind and body is the fact that what we describe as "the unconscious" from the internal viewpoint of subjectivity, appears to be co-extensive with that portion of physical space which is occupied by the body, when it is considered from the external, objective viewpoint. Because this implication seems strange, I will quote a lengthy passage in which Freud clarifies the situation:

> Many people, both inside and outside science, are satisfied with the assumption that consciousness alone is psychical; in that case nothing remains for psychology but to discriminate among psychical phenomena between perceptions, feelings, thought-processes and volitions. It is generally agreed, however, that these conscious processes do not form *unbroken se-*

> *quences* which are complete in themselves; there would thus be no alternative left to assuming that there are physical or somatic processes which are concomitant with the psychical ones and which we should necessarily have to recognize as *more complete* than the psychical sequences, since *some of them would have conscious processes parallel to them but others would not*. If so, it of course becomes plausible to lay the stress in psychology on these somatic processes, to see in *them* the essence of what is psychical and to look for some other assessment of the conscious processes. The majority of philosophers, however, as well as many other people, dispute this and declare that the idea of something psychical being unconscious is self-contradictory. But this is precisely what psycho-analysis is obliged to assert. . . . *It explains the supposedly somatic concomitant phenomena as being what is truly psychical*, and thus in the first instance disregards the quality of consciousness. [Freud, 1940a, pp. 57–158; emphasis added]

This passage enables us to understand better what Freud had in mind when he defined the concept of drive as "a concept on the frontier between the mental and the somatic" (1915c). The unconscious processes that underlie the phenomena of consciousness can clearly be represented *either* as psychic states *or* as somatic states, depending upon one's point of view.[4] However, since we perceive the body as a whole and we perceive the mind in broken sequences, psychoanalysis completes the mental sequence by *inferring* the "missing" subjective states (and attempting to make them conscious).

I hope it is clear that Freud did *not* believe that the unconscious portion of the mind is "really" or "in fact" the body. Rather, in agreement with Kant's philosophy, he assumed that there is a unitary underlying "thing", which exists independently of our conscious perceptions, which we *represent* in two fundamentally dif-

---

[4] See also Freud (1925e): "The overwhelming majority of philosophers regard as mental only the phenomena of consciousness. . . . Everything else that may take place in the "mind"—an entity so hard to grasp—is relegated by them to the *organic determinants* of mental processes. . . . What, then, can a philosopher say to a theory which, like psycho-analysis, asserts that on the contrary what is mental is in itself *unconscious* and that consciousness is only a quality which may or may not accrue to a particular mental act" (p. 216; emphasis added).

ferent ways on the two surfaces of consciousness. We perceive this unconscious "thing" externally as the body (as "an anatomical preparation"), and we perceive it internally as our subjective states of mind (as "our acts of consciousness"). But the unconscious "thing" itself—the metaphysical stuff that we are made of and the metapsychological forces that *drive* us—can never be known directly. These obscure, non-perceptual entities are therefore best described as lying "on the frontier between the mental and the somatic" (Freud, 1915c).[5]

This profound philosophy—at least in so far as it concerns external perception—has been a basic premise of sensory physiology for almost two centuries. It was imparted to Freud by von Brücke, who (together with his friend and colleague von Helmholtz) learned it from the great physiologist Johannes Müller, who in turn was influenced directly by Kant. I am not aware of a single modern physiologist who disputes the scientific implications of Kant's philosophy; it is universally accepted that the sensory apparatus must interpose its own inherent properties between our perceptions of reality and reality itself. Accordingly, it is implicitly accepted by sensory physiologists that what we perceive consciously is always a *model* of reality—a "construction" (see, for example, Zeki, 1993). Freud merely applied this same principle to the internal surface of consciousness.

Due to the importance of this extended conception of Kant's philosophy for my argument, I would like to quote a lengthy passage from Freud, in which he states it explicitly:

> The psycho-analytic assumption of unconscious mental activity appears to us . . . as *an extension of the corrections undertaken*

---

[5] Cf. Freud's remark to Groddeck (letter dated 5 June 1917): "the unconscious is the proper mediator between the somatic and the mental, perhaps the long-sought 'missing link'" (Groddeck, 1977, p. 38).

I am using the term "unconscious" in a purely descriptive sense in this chapter. The empirical fact that some unconscious processes are readily transformed into conscious ones while others resist such transformation—and the theoretical notion that some unconscious processes are incapable of ever becoming subjectively conscious—are immaterial to my general argument. I will argue that unconscious processes of the latter (absolute) variety can only be realized perceptually on the external surface of consciousness.

> *by Kant* of our views of external perception. Just as Kant warned us not to overlook the fact that our [external] perceptions are subjectively conditioned and must not be regarded as identical with what is perceived though unknowable, so psycho-analysis warns us not to equate [internal] perceptions by means of consciousness with the unconscious mental processes which are their object. Like the physical, the psychical is not necessarily in *reality* what it *appears* to be. [Freud, 1915e, p. 171; emphasis added][6]

On this basis, Freud stated the scientific goals of psychoanalysis as follows:

> In our science as in the others the problem is the same: behind the attributes (qualities) of the object under examination which are presented directly to our perception, *we have to discover something else which is more independent of the particular receptive capacity of our sense organs* and *which approximates more closely to what may be supposed to be the real state of affairs*. We have no hope of being able to reach the latter itself, since it is evident that everything new that we have inferred must nevertheless be translated back into the language of our perceptions, from which it is simply impossible to free ourselves. But herein lies the very nature and limitation of our science. It is as though we were to say in physics: "If we could see clearly enough we should find that what appears to be a solid body is made up of particles of such and such shape and size occupying such and such relative positions." In the meantime we try to increase the efficiency of our sense organs to the furthest possible extent by artificial aids; but it may be expected that all such efforts will fail to affect the ultimate outcome. Reality in itself will always remain "unknowable". [Freud, 1940a, p. 196; emphasis added]

I apologize for quoting all these obscure passages. This was necessary in order for me to sketch a general conceptual framework, which will now enable us to tackle the difficult problem of the relationship between affect and the body.

---

[6] I am indebted to Rosalie Sand for drawing my attention to the fact that Kant himself held this view. Freud was therefore not so much extending as adopting Kant's philosophy.

Affect arises from within

I am not saying anything unexpected when I assert that our emotions arise from within us. However, to be more precise, I should say that because the psychic manifestations of affect are registered on the internal surface of consciousness (because they are felt subjectively), we assume that they arise from within us. In accordance with the general framework outlined above, perceptions of this (subjective) type are considered to be representations of real happenings occurring in the unconscious portion of the mind. The unconscious is not a physical place. However, since it is conceptualized as the essence of the subject, it is assumed to exist within us. Moreover, since we do not perceive our feelings as material objects (via our external sensory organs), we do not attribute to them an independent, objective existence. Those of us who do perceive our feelings as physical objects have projected them onto the external surface of consciousness from the psychic world within us; and this form of projection is pathological (cf. the "bizarre objects" of Bion, 1957).

Here we must take care not to confuse the essential mechanism of affect with the complex processes that *trigger* that mechanism. Affect occurs within a complex causal matrix that includes both internal and external events. Although the perception of an unexpected external event (e.g. a bolt of lightning) may trigger an appropriate internal response (e.g. a fright), the internal response is not a perception of the external event (the fright is not a perception of the lightning). The emotion is a perception of an *internal* process, which was triggered by the external process, which was perceived as an external event. We therefore say that affect arises from within, notwithstanding the fact that the psychic mechanism of affect may be triggered from without (contra Sandler, 1972).[7]

---

[7] The subjective mechanism of affect is not inconsistent with its protocommunicative function. One perceives the emotional state (or emotional communications) of other people through the mechanism of empathy [*Einfühlung*], which reproduces the inner state of the other within the self. The emotions of the other are, therefore, paradoxically perceived (and often enough misperceived) by looking *inward*. This origin is not always apparent to the perceiving subject. Infants, and to a greater or lesser extent all of us, probably perceive affects *as if* they come from without. Indeed, it is a developmental achievement

The situation is less complicated with respect to the *somatic* manifestations of affect. These (e.g. palpitations associated with fright) are unequivocally located within us. They are registered on that portion of the surface of consciousness which represents our own bodily states. Scientific studies of other bodies similar to our own ("anatomical preparations") have demonstrated conclusively that the somatic manifestations of affect are caused by internal physiological changes.

In accordance with the general conceptual framework outlined above, it is important to remind ourselves that the internal physiological changes that generate the somatic manifestations of affect are not literally identical with the internal unconscious happenings that generate subjective acts of consciousness. The visual, coenaesthetic, and other physical representations that we conventionally group together and call "my body" are *conscious* perceptions. Even though these perceptions possess all the substantive properties of matter, they are *perceptions* nonetheless. In accordance with Kant's philosophy, we believe that behind our perceptions of the physical body there lies something else—something that is "independent of the particular receptive capacity of our sense organs" (Freud, 1940a, p. 196), which corresponds to "the real state of affairs" (p. 196). It is this "something else" (which we perceive as "my body" from the viewpoint of objective perception) that is conceptually equivalent to the mental unconscious (which we perceive as "my self" from the viewpoint of subjective awareness). I perceive myself both as a body and as a self (as an object and as a subject); I am perceptually realized on both surfaces of my con-

---

to recognize the true state of affairs (i.e. that one's feelings may be triggered from without but actually arise from within).

Of interest in this respect is the synaesthesia of the normal infant. Evidently the primitive confusion between the inner and outer surfaces of consciousness that underlies projected (and introjected) affects initially extends also to the differentiation between the various external sensory modalities. Thus the baby might "see" something in response to a noise in just the same way as he might "see" something in response to an emotion (cf. Freud's paradigmatic wishful hallucination of the breast). The mature distinction between inner and outer states has obvious survival value, which probably explains the tenacity of dualist conceptions of the mind–body relation. This same distinction is the biological basis of the metapsychological functions of "reality testing" and "specific action".

sciousness. *The psychic and the somatic manifestations of affect are therefore two ways of representing the same underlying thing.* The unknowable internal process that we call "affect" is registered on *both* perceptual surfaces *simultaneously;* it is perceived as an emotion (e.g. a fright) on the internal surface of consciousness and as a somatic state (e.g. palpitations) on the external surface of consciousness. This simple fact explains why affect is both an essentially subjective state and something that is inextricably connected with the body.

Therefore, when we say that affect arises from within, we are not saying that affect arises from the body. (This is the James–Lange theory of emotion.)[8] Just as it would be a logical error to describe an emotion (e.g. a fright) as an internal perception of an external event (e.g. of lightning), it would likewise be a logical error to describe an emotion as a psychic perception of a somatic state. Just as a smell cannot be a perception of a taste, *the object of an internal perception cannot be an external perception.* Both forms of perception represent something *else,* which is *unconscious* in itself. Thus the viscera are not the internal world; they are an external (physical) presentation of the internal world. The internal world itself is unconscious.

Now, if we accept that affect is a perceptual feeling that arises from within, and that such perceptions are registered on the internal surface of consciousness, then the following additional conclusion seems justified. Just as vision, hearing, somatic sensation, taste, and smell are the primary sensory modalities through which we perceive the external (objective) world of material reality, *affect is the primary sensory modality through which we perceive the internal (subjective) world of psychic reality.*[9] These sensory modalities pro-

---

[8] The James–Lange theory has recently been revived by Damasio (1994; cf. Solms, 1997b).

[9] "Consciousness, which we look upon [as] a sense organ for the apprehension of psychical qualities, is capable . . . of receiving excitations from two directions. In the first place, it can receive excitations from the periphery of the whole apparatus, the perceptual system; and in addition to this, it can receive excitations of pleasure and unpleasure, which prove to be almost *the only psychical quality* attaching to transpositions of energy in the inside of the apparatus. All other processes in the [unconscious] are lacking in any psychical quality and so cannot be objects of consciousness, except in so far as they bring

vide the raw material for the envelope of consciousness, "from which it is simply impossible to free ourselves" (Freud, 1940a, p. 196). Just as the external senses represent aspects of reality to us in the form of sights, sounds, bodily sensations, tastes, and smells, so our internal sense organ represents an aspect of reality to us in the form of emotions. Moreover, just as each external sensory modality represents reality in the form of a particular qualitative range (e.g. the wavelength composition of light), so, too, the sense of affect has its own qualitative range. We conventionally calibrate this range in terms of relative degrees of pleasure and unpleasure. We may therefore consider pleasure and unpleasure to be the basic qualities of the sensory modality called affect.

What about ideas?

Of course, simple sensations of pleasure and unpleasure *combine* with other, externally derived perceptual qualities (and memories thereof) to produce more complex forms of emotion, such as envy and guilt. The complex emotions that we normally experience are in fact affect–idea complexes (cf. Brenner, 1974). Analogous arrangements exist for the other sensory modalities, none of which functions in isolation. Constantly conjoined innervations of the internal and various external sensory modalities produce *internal object* or "selfobject" presentations (such as "good breast"/ "bad breast"). The permanent traces of these innervations are structuralized in the ego and superego, which have a guiding influence over all subsequent experience.[10] These structuralized representations of previous perceptual experiences are accessible to both external and internal sources of activation (e.g. recognizing, phantasying). They are also subject to modification throughout

pleasure or unpleasure to perception" (Freud, 1900a, p. 574; emphasis added). "A feeling seems to be the inner perception of an instinctual cathexis" (Freud to Jung, 27 August 1907—McGuire, 1974, p. 80).

[10] This is not to deny the existence of innate ideas, which, nevertheless, can only acquire their representational quality through external experiences (cf. Bion's 1962 theory of "pre-conception", with which I am in total agreement).

life, from both external and internal sources. It would therefore be a serious mistake to conflate the *primary sensory modality* of internal perception (i.e. affect) with the whole range of internal processes that constitute the *lived experience* of psychic reality (recognizing, remembering, thinking, phantasying, dreaming, etc.). In the natural course of events, affect occurs in continuous combination with these more complex ideational processes and with other (external) primary perceptual processes. However, for scientific purposes—just as sensory physiologists isolate vision, hearing, somatic sensation, taste, and smell from the rich tapestry of lived perceptual life—so we, too, may isolate affect from the mental field within which it naturally occurs.

The scientific task

According to the formulation I quoted earlier, it is the basic task of science to probe the limits of the envelope of consciousness "to the furthest possible extent by artificial aids" (Freud, 1940a, p. 196), in order to "arrive at what is described as an 'understanding' of the field of natural phenomena in question" (p. 158):

> Behind the attributes (qualities) of the object under examination which are presented directly to our perception, we have to discover *something else* which is more independent of the particular receptive capacity of our sense organs and which approximates more closely to what may be supposed to be *the real state of affairs.* [Freud, 1940a, p. 196; emphasis added]

Just as physicists and physiologists are not content merely to describe and classify the various attributes of our external sensory modalities and the objects that they generate but, rather, want to know what lies behind them, so we psychoanalysts too want to know what lies behind the surface attributes of our internal sensory perceptions. *We are therefore charged with the scientific task of developing observational aids that will enable us to arrive at an "understanding" of the unconscious happenings that lie behind the attributes of subjective consciousness, and of the vehicles by which those happenings are conveyed to us.* It is therefore not sufficient to answer the question, "what is affect?" with the statement, "affect is a primary sensory modality". This is merely a *taxonomic* statement, which "discriminate[s] among psychical phenomena" (Freud, 1940a, p. 196). We must go further and attempt to comprehend the "real state of affairs" that *lies behind* emotional feelings.

Freud was the first to attempt this basic scientific task, using the "artificial aid" of the psychoanalytic technique. There is no need for me to provide a detailed account of his findings here, nor of the theory of affect that he based upon them (more or less detailed accounts of which can be found in Brenner, 1974; Brierly, 1937; Jacobson, 1953; Laplanche & Pontalis, 1973; Lewin, 1965; Rapaport, 1953; Sandler, 1972; Solms & Nersessian, 1999). I will just state the most essential conclusions arising from his pioneering investigations. Freud believed that the external sensory surface of consciousness registered two types of motor discharge. One of these was muscular action, which alters the external environment; the other was "secretory processes", which result in "internal changes".[11] From the viewpoint of metapsychology, these "internal changes" are quantitative in nature. (Freud defined these unconscious mechanisms in *quantitative* terms in order to distinguish them from perceptual *qualia*.) His basic metapsychological proposition in this regard was that internal discharges of psychic quantities—which alter the level of unbound[12] quantities within the mind—are perceived qualitatively in the form of emotions (i.e. they are registered in the pleasure–unpleasure series on the internal surface of consciousness).[13] On this basis, Freud suspected that unpleasure corresponds to an increase and pleasure to a diminution in the level of unbound quantity, but he was uncertain about

[11] "Affectivity manifests itself essentially in motor (secretory and vasomotor) discharge resulting in an (internal) alteration of the subject's own body without reference to the external world; motility in actions is designed to effect changes in the external world" (Freud, 1915e, p. 179 n). In this passage Freud is describing affect from a purely physiological viewpoint.

[12] "Unbound" quantities are freely discharged; "bound" quantities are inhibited (see Laplanche & Pontalis, 1973).

[13] We may add that these unconscious changes simultaneously manifest themselves *physiologically*—on the *external* surface of consciousness—as sensations of the motor discharges described above.

the precise mechanism of this correspondence.[14] Finally, Freud recognized that affect can also arise (in a "tamed" form) as a *signal* from the *expectation* of a quantitative change (due to the structural influence of memory; see above). This is our classical metapsychological "understanding" of the "real state of affairs" that lies behind affective experience.

Much of the criticism of Freud's theory of affect has been directed at its quasi-physiological (quantitative) postulates. I hope that it is clear from what I have said already that *it is in fact incorrect to suppose that Freud's quantitative postulates refer to physiological processes* (although they are of necessity *correlated* with physiological phenomena). Freud used an abstract (quantitative) language in his theory of affect (and in the whole of his metapsychology) in order to describe something that needed to be "independent of the particular receptive capacity of our sense organs" (Freud, 1940a, p. 196). Recent advances in our psychoanalytic understanding of affect have tended to describe the underlying processes from the representational viewpoint of the experiencing self, usually in relation to an object (i.e. in terms of "unconscious phantasies", "states of mind", etc.). This approach to metapsychology[15] is purely psychological in the sense that it describes psychic reality purely in the

---

[14] "We . . . relate pleasure and unpleasure to the quantity of excitation that is present in the mind but is not in any way "bound"; and we relate them in such a manner that unpleasure corresponds to an increase in the quantity of excitation and pleasure to a diminution. *What we are implying by this is not a simple relation between the strength of the feelings of pleasure and unpleasure and the corresponding modifications in the quantity of excitation*; least of all—in view of all we have been taught by psychophysiology—are we suggesting any directly proportional ratio: the factor that determines the feeling is probably the amount of increase or diminution in a given period of time. Experiment might possibly play a part here; but it is not advisable for us analysts to go into the problem further so long as our way is not pointed by definite observations" (Freud, 1920g, p. 8, emphasis added [see also p. 63]; 1924c, p. 160). These important remarks are often overlooked by contemporary critics of Freud's affect theory (Schore, 1994; Stern, 1990; cf. Solms, 1997c).

[15] I use the term "metapsychology" to refer to any systematic account of unconscious mental life. The term is often treated as if it were synonymous with Freud's model of the mind. This is incorrect. Freud's formulations are but one among many possible ways of describing the unknowable reality that lies beyond consciousness; they constitute *a* metapsychology, not *the* metapsychology. Unless we possess *a* metapsychology, we cannot have a basic science of the mind.

language of subjective experience. Since this is the natural (intersubjective) language of the psychoanalytic consulting-room, it narrows the gap between our theoretical concepts and models and our clinical observations and technique. However, when it comes to affect theory, this approach to metapsychology has the disadvantage of conflating primary *perceptions* of internal reality with secondary (structuralized) *representations* of the object world—in other words, it conflates the ego's perception of the id (emotions proper) with its perception of its own contents and those of the superego (the ideational processes associated with emotions). The representational schools also blur the fundamental distinction that Freud drew between the "particular receptive capacity of our sense organs" and the "real state of affairs" that lies behind them. This can result in confusions between description and explanation (Brierly, 1951), which has been the cause of so much pseudo-controversy in psychoanalysis.

It should always be possible—at least in principle—to reduce a naturalistic description of a subjective experience (whether it be conscious or unconscious) to an abstract explanatory account of the mechanism by which that experience was generated. The two approaches (description and explanation) are clearly complementary. Indeed, they form the very bedrock of the scientific method, in which observation (or description) acts as a constant constraint and corrective to theory (or explanation).

In this respect, the classical (abstract) approach to metapsychology, with its clear distinction between the underlying reality on the one hand and the two classes of perceptual realization on the other, has an unexpected but highly significant advantage: *it is accessible—at least in principle—to empirical correction through both psychic and physical research.* An adequate theory of the mechanism of affect (an adequate explanation) should square with both the psychic and the physical realizations of that mechanism (both empirical descriptions), since *the two perceptual viewpoints describe one and the same thing*. For historical reasons, this advantage of the classical approach has remained for the most part unexploited (see Solms & Saling, 1986). However, if one recalls the moral about the blind men and the elephant, it is apparent what a significant advantage it can be. Perhaps this is the reason why Freud always enthusiastically anticipated a time when advances in the physical sciences would make it possible to study the interior of the human subject—and the unconscious forces that drive it—also from the viewpoint of its anatomical and physiological realizations (see Freud, 1905c, p. 148; 1905d, p. 168; 1905e, p. 113; 1906a, pp. 278–279; 1914c, p. 78; 1913j, p. 182; 1915e, pp. 167–168, 174–75; 1916–17a, pp. 388–389, 436; 1920g, p. 60; 1926d, p. 152–153; 1931b, p. 240; 1933a, p. 154; 1939a, p. 97; 1940a, p. 182).

The anatomy and physiology of affect

Psychoanalysts are painfully aware of the fact that the external surface of consciousness is better adapted than the internal surface to the requirements of natural scientific observation.[16] One need only think of the pejorative connotations in science of the word "subjective" to be reminded of the basis for this fact. We console ourselves with the view that this is an unavoidable consequence of the manner in which the mental instrument is constructed. We say that the mind is inherently biased towards external (material) reality,[17] and we rightfully assert that this should not deter us from studying its internal workings, by whatever methods seem appropriate to the task. Nevertheless, we cannot deny that numerous advantages attach to the study of external objects. These advantages are so obvious that I will not attempt to enumerate them. What is important is the fact that these advantages facilitated the development of observational technologies ("artificial aids") in the physical sciences which are unimaginable in our (psychic) field. These advances have yielded dramatic new insights into the nature of reality, which have had significant practical applications (even in the field of psychiatry)— the "undreamt-of possibilities" mentioned in footnote 1.

---

[16] "The deficiencies in our description would probably vanish if we were already in a position to replace the psychological terms by physiological and chemical ones" (Freud, 1920g, p. 60).

[17] "All of our attention is directed to the outside, whence dangers threaten and satisfactions beckon. From the inside, we want only to be left in peace. So if someone tries to turn our awareness inward, in effect twisting its neck round, then our whole organization resists—just as, for example, the oesophagus and urethra resist any attempt to reverse their normal direction of passage" (Freud, 1994a [1929], p. 117).

Against this background, I will now summarize what has been learnt about affect from the viewpoint of its physiological (material) realization since Freud's death. I have space only to describe selected aspects of these findings, in a very schematic way. I will link the physical findings to Freud's classical theory (in footnotes to the text) in order to clarify the relationship between the classical theory and this new data, and thereby to facilitate direct neuroscientific research on the metapsychology of affect.

As I have said already, the mental apparatus that generates affect cannot be perceived directly. However, it can be represented objectively in the form of "its bodily organ and scene of action, the brain (or nervous system)" (Freud, 1940a, p. 144). The brain (or nervous system) is the material form in which the mental apparatus is presented to the external surface of consciousness. Although this "anatomical preparation" is not within the scientific domain of psychoanalysis, it still is of interest to us for the reason that it describes the (unconscious) mental apparatus from a different point of view. Approaching the question, "what is affect?", from this point of view enables us to consider the anatomy and physiology of our subject. This approach has proved immensely fruitful in advancing our understanding of the *external* sensory modalities via the study of sensory organs and has revealed a great deal about the "real state of affairs" that lies behind externally derived qualia.

I will preface my overview of the anatomy and physiology of affect with some general remarks on the functional organization of the nervous system as a whole. My aim is to provide an overview of how perceptual and motor processes in general are represented anatomically and physiologically, before discussing the distinctive physical correlates of the particular modality of consciousness known as affect.[18]

---

[18] In this overview I am concerned primarily with the elementary sensory-motor functions of the brain, since these are the most relevant to my discussion of *the perceptual nature of affect*. Higher functions (such as remembering, thinking, and phantasying) are regulated by extremely complex mechanisms, the anatomy and physiology of which I have discussed elsewhere (Solms, 1996). These higher mechanisms subserve the representational concomitants of affect, which are barely discussed here. They also participate in the "taming" of affect (and the binding of the primary process in general)—likewise, scarcely discussed here.

The nervous system is divided into two great functional components. One of these divisions processes stimuli derived from the external environment, and the other processes stimuli derived from the internal milieu of the body (Figure 1). The externally oriented division projects to the outer surface of the cerebrum. It is connected with the environment by a series of cranial and spinal extensions, which terminate in sensory receptors and motor effectors. The internally oriented division forms the core of the brain. It is connected with the viscera through the spinal cord and various (non-nervous) circulatory mechanisms. The two great functional divisions of the nervous system process stimuli in somewhat different ways; I discuss these two divisions separately.

EXTRAPERSONAL SPACE

IDIOTYPIC CORTEX

1: sensory-motor areas

HOMOTYPICAL ISOCORTEX

2: modality-specific (unimodal association) areas

3: high-order (heteromodal) association areas

PARALIMBIC CORTEX

[3] temporal pole, caudal orbitofrontal cortex, anterior insula, cingulate, parahippocampal gyri

LIMBIC ALLOCORTEX

[2] hippocampus, piriform cortex

LIMBIC CORTICOID TISSUE

[1] basal forebrain nuclei, amygdala

HYPOTHALAMUS

INTERNAL MILIEU

FIGURE 1. Classification of human cortical tissues (after Mesulam, 1985)

The outer surface of the cerebrum

The outer surface of the cerebrum (Figure 2a) is conventionally subdivided into two major structuro-functional units. The first of these units—the posterior part—principally subserves perceptual and representational functions. The second unit—the anterior part—principally subserves motor and executive functions. I will call these the "perceptual" and "motor" units for short. These units are composed of three grades of cortical tissue. These are traditionally described as primary, secondary, and tertiary cortex. These three grades of cortex are differentiated on the basis of their cellular architecture (patterns of tissue morphology and connectivity.[19]

Neurones are the elementary structuro-functional units of the nervous system. Cortical neurones fire spontaneously, in the absence of perceptual stimulation or motor activity. This is called their "resting" rate of firing. External stimuli exert their effects on perceptual cortex by differentially altering the resting rate of neuronal activity. The stimuli are relayed to the cortex by the peripheral sensory receptors,[20] via a series of interconnected subcortical pathways. These subcortical relay systems are described as "modality-specific", for the reason that each relay-system subserves a specific sensory modality (Figure 2).[21] Each element in these systems propagates a selected parameter of physical change impinging on the external surface of the body (light, temperature, etc.).

---

[19] Various taxonomies have been proposed. The present account follows the relatively conservative classification of Mesulam (1985), who describes primary cortex as "idiotypic cortex" and secondary and tertiary cortex as "homotypical isocortex". He subdivides the latter into "modality-specific (unimodal) association" and "high-order (heteromodal) association" types (see Figure 1).

[20] Freud (1950 [1895]) described the peripheral receptors as "Q screens". He later subsumed them into the "system *Pcpt.*" (Freud, 1900a), which—together with the revised "Cs." system of his second topographical model—eventually became the superficial surface of the structural "ego" (Freud, 1923b).

[21] See Brodal (1981) for anatomical details. Freud (1950 [1895]) described these relay systems as the ϕ system of neurones. He argued that the myriad transformations that peripheral stimuli undergo during their passage through this system give material expression to the impossibility of veridical object perception (Freud, 1891b, 1893c). The same principle applies to stimuli derived from the internal milieu (see fn. 29 below).

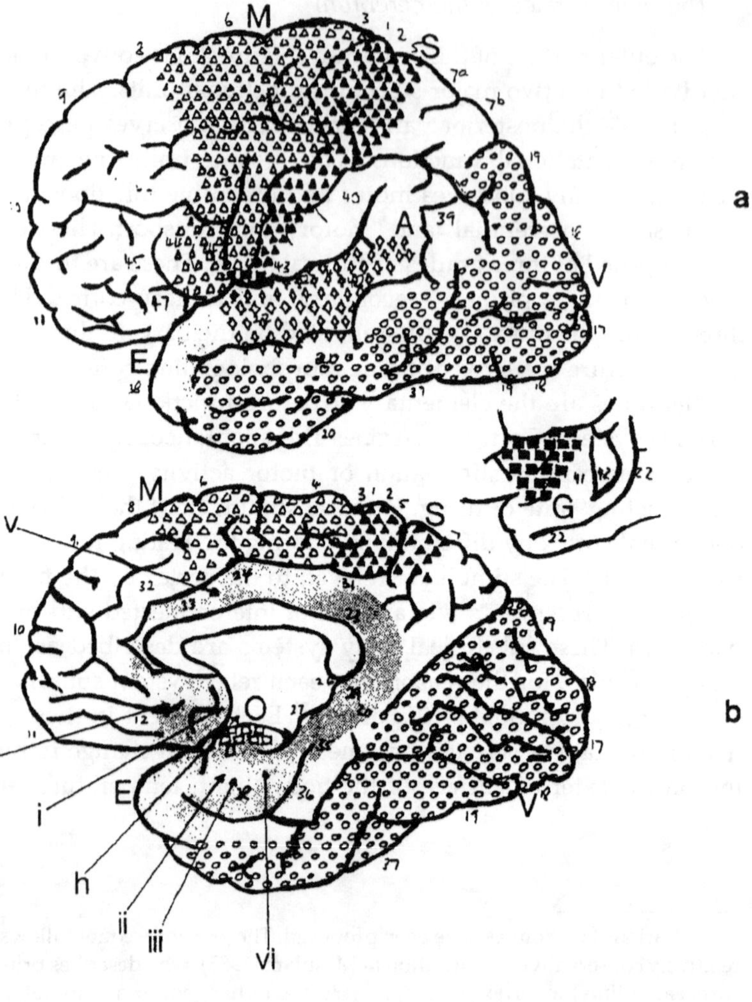

S = general somatosensory cortex; G = gustatory cortex; V = visual cortex; A = auditory cortex; O = olfactory cortex; E = emotional cortex; M = motor cortex; h = hypothalamic–pituitary complex; (i) = basal forebrain nuclei; (ii) = lateral amygdaloid complex (basolateral nuclei); (iii) = medial amygdaloid complex (cortical and central nuclei); (iv) = orbitofrontal cortex; (v) = cingulate gyrus; (vi) = hippocampal formation.

FIGURE 2. Schematic illustration of the anatomical distribution of modality-specific cortex, on (**a**) the external surface and (**b**) the internal surface of the human brain.

Each parameter causes physical changes in different peripheral receptors, which in turn cause neurones in the different relay-systems with which they are connected to fire at faster or slower rates. These discrete changes in the rates of spontaneous firing are conveyed, via the modality-specific pathways, to the primary cortical zones.[22] The range of changes within the physical parameters to which each pathway responds is represented *topographically* in the primary cortical zones attached to it—that is, the rate at which different neurones in the primary zones fire is altered in a topographically differentiated pattern. Changes at particular *places* within each primary zone represent the external changes within the parameter of reality to which that modality is sensitive. The primary zones themselves are distributed in a fixed topographic pattern over the posterior surface of the brain. Stimulation of the different zones (i.e. of different primary cortices) generates the basic modalities of external consciousness. A different modality is associated with each primary zone (Figure 2).[23] Through these simple contrivances, the rich diversity of external qualities (or those that the brain is capable of registering) is represented by way of a unitary quantitative parameter—namely, the rate of firing of neurones. The topographical pattern of differentiated firing at a

---

[22] See Mesulam (1985) for anatomical details. Freud (1950 [1895]) described these cortical zones as the ω system of neurones. He later subsumed them, too, into the "*Pcpt.–Cs.*" surface of the structural "ego" (1923b), on the basis of a substantial revision of his 1895 model (Letter 39, Freud, 1950 [1895]).

Modality-specific relays do not project exclusively to primary cortical zones. I am omitting numerous anatomical and physiological details in this simplified and schematic account.

[23] Freud (1950 [1895]) described these modalities as "qualities". We now distinguish at least ten basic qualia: light, sound, touch, pain, temperature, vibration, joint sense, muscle sense, taste, and odour. Touch, pain, temperature, vibration, joint sense, and muscle sense are grouped together under the rubric of "general somatic sensation" (see Brodal, 1981, for physiological and anatomical details). Moreover, there are numerous subsidiary qualities within each sensory division. In relation to light, for example, modern neuroscientists distinguish between orientation (form), wavelength (colour), and vector (movement). Each submodality has its own anatomical representation within the primary zones (see Zeki, 1993, for physiological and anatomical details). This is an example of how physiological and anatomical studies have advanced our knowledge of "the real state of affairs" that lies behind consciousness awareness (Freud 1940a, p. 196).

given moment in time is the physical equivalent of a moment of external conscious awareness.[24]

The topographically distributed pattern of neuronal firing in primary cortical neurones is propagated to secondary and tertiary cortex (and the selected subcortical nuclei with which they are connected) along parallel but partly interconnected channels.[25] These dedicated channels transcribe and retranscribe the primary topographical patterns according to myriad functional criteria, which differentially alter the spontaneous firing patterns in these regions. They thereby categorize aspects of the original stimuli into progressively more complex patterns, which display diminishing modal specificity.[26] Nevertheless, *the categories are processed in dis-*

---

[24] This topographic conception of quality differs from Freud's (1950 [1895]) formulation, which correlated quality with the differentiated frequencies (or "periods") of sensory stimuli. However, the two conceptions are not exclusive, as the topographic conception concerns central processes, while the periodic conception concerns peripheral processes. It is also important to recognize that the *stream* of consciousness corresponds to a temporal process, whereby rapid sequences of attentional (ψ) cathexes sample the current state of the ω neurones. This provides a metapsychological explanation of the sense of time, which is a fundamental property of consciousness (cf. Freud 1950 [1895], p. 337; 1920g, p. 28; 1925a, p. 231; 1925h, p. 238; 1933a, p. 76; 1940a, p. 159). This sampling process probably correlates with the "40-Hertz oscillations" described in recent physiological research (Crick & Koch, 1990).

[25] See Mesulam (1985) for anatomical details. Freud (1950 [1895]) described these cortico-subcortical channels as the "ψ pallium". He later subsumed them into the unconscious "mnemic" systems (Freud, 1900a) and the unconscious portion of the structural "ego" (1923b). Processes occurring in these systems can become conscious if they are brought into associative connection with the ω system (i.e. the system *Pcpt.–Cs.*).

Recent studies suggest that perceptual consciousness correlates with primary cortical stimulation, together with a process of continuous "back projection" or "re-entry" from secondary cortex (see Edelman, 1990, and Crick, 1994, for accessible reviews). In terms of Freud's (1950 [1895]) model, this corresponds to omega "indications of reality", coupled with a process of psi discharge into omega (see also the concept of attentional "hypercathexis").

[26] "As you know, I am working on the assumption that our psychical mechanism has come about by a process of stratification: the material present in the shape of memory-traces is from time to time subjected to a rearrangement in accordance with fresh circumstances—is, as it were, transcribed" (Freud 1950 [1892–1899], Letter 52 [1895]). These higher-order transcriptions further emphasize Freud's (1891b, 1893c) arguments concerning the non-veridical nature of conscious perception (cf. fn. 21).

crete areas and are propagated along relatively circumscribed channels within the perceptual cortex. Thus, although they no longer represent activity in the primary sensory receptors in a purely somatotopic fashion, they nevertheless still display a high degree of *functional* topographic specificity. Accordingly, modern authors identify innumerable material-specific "modules" and "pathways" within perceptual cortex. A recent model of the interconnecting modules and pathways subserving visual perception, for example, specifies 47 anatomically separate units of analysis (Felleman & van Essen, 1991; see also Zeki, 1993). On this basis, Mesulam (1985) has aptly described the functions of perceptual cortex as *"channel-dependent"*.

Perceptual cortex ultimately conveys the results of its information-processing activities to motor cortex, via cortical and subcortical connections.[27] The functions of the motor unit are also "channel-dependent"—that is, external influences upon spontaneous neuronal activity in all perceptual and motor cortex are propagated along dedicated (functionally discrete) modules and pathways. However, in general, motor cortex reverses the direction of the processing sequence that occurred in the perceptual unit. It progressively retranscribes complex, material-specific firing patterns into simpler, modality-specific arrangements through tertiary and secondary motor cortex. It appears that it simultaneously combines parallel processes into serial ones. (Serial processes, which necessarily involve a degree of selection, are fundamental to the mechanism of attention and many other executive mechanisms; cf. footnote 24.) These arrangements are then retranscribed into basic patterns of discharge in primary motor neurones. The final patterns of discharge innervate peripheral muscular activity in a somatotopic arrangement. The topographic pattern of neuronal firing is thus transformed back into *external* physical events.

---

[27] See Mesulam (1985) for anatomical details. These cortical channels (and their associated subcortical nuclei) are also included in the "ψ pallium" (cf. fn. 25). Freud (1900a) later subsumed them into the system *"Pcs."*. Processes occurring in this system, too, can become conscious if they are brought into associative connection with the "system *Cs.*". The *Cs.* system was later subsumed into the combined system *"Pcpt.–Cs."*, which seems also to include the motor apparatus of the structural "ego", although this was not explicitly stated by Freud (1923b).

It is important to recognize that *the body itself is a physical object from the viewpoint of externally oriented cortex*. In fact, it could be said that all primary cortex ultimately represents the body (including its specialized sensory organs).[28]

The inner surface of the brain

The influence of the internal milieu of the body on the brain (or nervous system) is more important than that of the external environment for the purposes of the present discussion. This influence is primarily brought to bear on the internal cortical surface (Figure 2b). However, before discussing the direct influence that the body exerts upon this (internal) surface, I will briefly mention its indirect impact upon the external cortical zones.

I said earlier that neurones in the externally oriented parts of the brain fire spontaneously, at a "resting" rate, in the absence of perceptual stimulation or motor activity. I should have qualified this statement by saying that they only fire spontaneously if the body within which they are situated is *alive*—in other words, the "spontaneous" firing of neurones does have quasi-representational content. It represents the (living) *state of the body*, of which the brain is but a part (cf. Damasio, 1994, 1999). This background rate of firing changes in accordance with changes in the state of the body. The rate of perceptual-motor neuronal firing is therefore influenced not only by events in the external environment, but also by internal events occurring within the body. These vital influences are communicated to the brain both by non-nervous mechanisms (discussed below) that terminate centrally in a region known as the hypothalamus (Figure 2b: h) and via a series of ganglia and nuclei.[29]

---

[28] "The ego is first and foremost a bodily ego; it is not merely a surface entity, but is itself the projection of a surface. (I.e. the ego is ultimately derived from bodily sensations, chiefly from those springing from the surface of the body. . . .) If we wish to find an anatomical analogy for it we can best identify it with the 'cortical homunculus' of the anatomists" (Freud, 1923b, p. 26 & n. 1).

[29] The preganglionic visceral nuclei, sympathetic and parasympathetic ganglia of the spinal cord, periaqueductal grey, nucleus locus coeruleus, raphe nuclei, nucleus of the solitary tract, and reticular formation (Brodal, 1981). Cf. fn. 21 above.

The patterned firing rates of hypothalamic neurones respond directly to metabolic and chemical changes in the internal milieu. Changes in these physiological parameters are then propagated upwards to the cortex. On this basis, higher cerebral activity is influenced by changes in the state of the body.[30]

However, these influences are not propagated to the cortex along discrete channels—they are not "channel-dependent". They are communicated via a system of deep nuclei (many of which are source-nuclei for single neurotransmitters) with *diffuse* cortical (and spinal) projections.[31] They are also transmitted by peptides and the hormonal secretions of the pituitary gland (which circulate throughout the body).[32] These neurotransmitters, peptides, and

---

[30] "The derivation and original biological significance of the primary brain are not known to anatomists; according to our theory, it would, to put it plainly, be a *sympathetic ganglion*. Here is a first possibility of testing our theory upon factual material" (Freud, 1950 [1895], p. 303).

[31] These nuclei include (in addition to the hypothalamus itself), the intralaminar group of thalamic nuclei (which project diffusely to widespread cortical regions), the cholinergic neurones of the basal forebrain nuclei (which project to the entire cortical surface), serotonergic neurones in the brainstem raphe nuclei (which project to the entire cortical surface), the cholinergic neurones in the pontomesencephalic reticular formation (which project to the entire thalamus and, to a lesser extent, the entire cortical surface), the noradrenergic neurones in the nucleus locus coeruleus complex (which project to the entire cortical surface), and the dopaminergic neurones in the substantia nigra and in the ventral tegmental area of Tsai (which innervate the entire striatum as well as many limbic, paralimbic, and heteromodal cortical areas). (Cf. Mesulam, 1985.) *It is no accident that the neurotransmitters sourced in these nuclei are the ones primarily targeted by the psychopharmacological agents listed in fn. 2 above.*

[32] The pituitary gland (which is controlled directly by the hypothalamus) discharges hormonal secretions into the cerebrospinal circulation. It therefore influences the brain through non-neurological means, and it treats the brain as just another bodily organ. (During embryogenesis, hormonal secretions also determine the gender of the brain and other organs.) The pituitary gland is functionally identical with Freud's (1950 [1895]) hypothetical "key" neurones, which secrete quantity from the "ψ nucleus" into the interior of the body (cf. Glick, 1966; Hoskins, 1936). This is the internal channel of "motor discharge" mentioned in the text above. Freud (1900a, p. 52) later assigned this "secretory" function to the system *Ucs*.

Freud (1950 [1895], p. 321) described the function of key neurones as follows (see also fn. 12 above): "The mechanism of this release [of unpleasure from the interior of the body] can be pictured as follows. Just as there are motor

hormones *modulate* cortical activity in a *modality-non-specific* way, by altering their spontaneous firing rate. These modulatory influences increase or decrease the firing thresholds of perceptual and motor neurones, but they are relatively *undifferentiated topographically*.[33] In other words, the somatic state of the organism generates *quantitative* changes on the external cortical surface; it does not generate specific sensory *qualities*. These quantitative changes alter the *level* (or state) of externally oriented consciousness, rather than its *contents*.[34] Changes in wakefulness, vigilance, and orientation are examples of changes in the level or state of consciousness. Due to this fundamental difference between internal and external influences upon the cerebral cortex, Mesulam (1985) has aptly described the internally generated influences as *"state-dependent"* functions. (This distinguishes them from the "channel-dependent" functions discussed previously.)

---

neurones which, when they are filled to a certain amount, conduct Q into the muscles and accordingly discharge it, so there must be 'secretory' neurones which, when they are excited, cause the generation in the interior of the body of something which operates as a stimulus upon the endogenous paths of conduction to ψ—neurones which thus influence the production of endogenous Q, and accordingly do not discharge Q but supply it in roundabout ways. We will call these [secretory] neurones 'key neurones'. . . . Support is lent to this puzzling but indispensable hypothesis by what happens in the case of sexual release. At the same time a suspicion forces itself on us that in both instances the endogenous stimuli consist of *chemical products*, of which there may be a considerable number".

It is important to recognize that key neurones discharge on the basis of (innate or acquired) memories. (The influence of memory upon affect is neglected here; cf. fn. 18).

[33] One important exception to this rule is provided by the fact that primary perceptual cortex is entirely free of such internal modulatory influences. In other words, primary cortical functions are not modulated by the somatic state. Cf. Freud's oft-repeated assertion that the systems subserving perception and those subserving memory must remain functionally independent (Freud, 1895d, 1900a, 1920g, 1925a, 1950 [1895]).

[34] The internally generated (quantitative) aspect of consciousness is sometimes described as "non-specific", to contrast it with modality-specific consciousness. Freud (1950a [1895/96]) attributed this aspect of consciousness to transfers of "Q η" (see especially Letter 39, Freud 1950 [1895], which stipulates that *all* Q η is endogenous). Freud subsequently described Q η as a *"quota of affect"*, and he later subsumed it into the general economic concept of "psychical energy".

I have said that indirect somatic influences on external consciousness are purely quantitative influences, for the reason that they do not generate modality-specific perceptual qualities.[35] However, the *internally* oriented division of the brain does possess a primary "modality-specific" zone of its own, with its own afferent receptor organs. This cortical zone lies deep within the brain's interior. It is connected directly with the hypothalamus. It forms part of a larger system known as the "limbic system" (Figure 2: i–vi).[36] The limbic system (together with the nuclei and ganglia listed in footnote 29) is—in my view—*the internal sensory organ of the brain.*[37] In a manner directly analogous to externally oriented cortex, limbic cortex is divided into three morphological grades. These

---

[35] A second system of corticopetal spinal neurones does represent some internal organs of the body on the external cerebral surface. However, these connections are relatively scanty, and the resultant somatic sensations are rather vague and distorted. (See Brodal, 1981, for details.) These connections provide the anatomical basis for the specific somatic sensations that accompany basic emotions.

It is important to note once again (contra the James–Lange theory of affect) that emotions are not subjective perceptions of these physical sensations, which are *themselves* perceptions. Emotion is not a perception of a perception—it is a perception of an unconscious internal process. This process is *also* perceived externally (albeit vaguely) as somatic sensation. For this reason, emotions typically co-occur with somatic sensations, but the two classes of perception are distinct. Damasio (1994) neglects this distinction (cf. fn. 8).

[36] The limbic system includes (in addition to the hypothalamus), the corticoid, allocortical, and paralimbic structures listed in Figure 1, the limbic striatum (i.e. the olfactory tubercle and nucleus accumbens), the limbic pallidum, the ventral tegmental area of Tsai, the habenula and the limbic and paralimbic nuclei of the thalamus (medial MD, P_m, AD, AV, AM, LD, and midline nuclei). Cf. Mesulam (1985).

The subcortical limbic nuclei (together with the nuclei listed in fns 25 and 27) correspond to the "ψ nucleus" in Freud's (1950 [1895]) model. The ψ nucleus was subsumed into the "system *Ucs.*" in Freud's later metapsychology (1900a). The cortical components of the limbic system are to be equated with the surface of the ω system, which abutted on the "ψ" system. This later became the internal surface of the system *Pcpt.–Cs.* and was therefore subsequently subsumed into the structural ego. Curiously, however, Freud sometimes described this surface as a part of the id (e.g. 1940a, p. 198).

[37] Cf. Freud's final remark on the subject of affect: "it is hard to say, to be sure, by what means and with the help of *what sensory terminal organs* these perceptions [of pleasure and unpleasure] come about" (1940a, p. 198; emphasis added).

can be described as primary, secondary, and tertiary limbic cortex. Primary limbic cortex is "corticoid" tissue; secondary limbic cortex is "allocortical" tissue; tertiary limbic cortex is "paralimbic" tissue (see Figure 1).

Primary limbic cortex is found in two regions: in the basal forebrain[38] and in the amygdaloid complex (Figure 2b: i, ii). *The conscious qualities that are generated by stimulation of these primitive cortical zones may therefore be described as the primary perceptual modality through which internal quantitative changes are registered in consciousness.* The conscious qualities generated by stimulation of secondary and tertiary limbic zones (see Figure 1) may be regarded as *more complex forms of affect*. Examples of simple and complex affects are described below. In addition to psychic *qualities* (principally of affect, but also of smell and reminiscence),[39] stimulation of limbic regions also generates *somatic (autonomic and endocrine) changes* and *instinctual and reflex behaviours.*[40] These are the two forms of motor discharge (internal and external discharge) that are associated with limbic stimulation.

I will now very briefly summarize the psychological and behavioural effects of limbic stimulation (see Panksepp, 1985, for a more detailed review). The anatomical locations of the circuits that I describe have proved quite similar in all mammalian species, including man.

A central hypothesis of this chapter—namely that *affect is the primary perceptual modality for internally generated stimuli*—is well supported by the fact that stimulation of the two primary limbic zones (basal forebrain and amygdaloid complex) generate *pleasure* and *unpleasure*, respectively.

- Stimulation of the basal forebrain (septal area and substantia inominata: Figure 2: i) generates *sexual delight and orgiastic sen-*

---

[38] In the septal area and the region that used to be described as the substantia inominata.

[39] The association between affect and smell is due to the close anatomical proximity of the primary cortical zones subserving these modalities, which, in turn, probably reflects a close phylogenetic association. The connection between affect and reminiscence is discussed in fn. 46 below.

[40] They are associated with what Freud described as "internal changes" and "innate hysterical attacks" (1926d, p. 133).

sations. These subjective qualia are accompanied by genital engorgement (internal discharge) and copulatory behaviour (external discharge).[41]

- Stimulation of the lateral parts of the amygdaloid complex (basolateral nuclei: Figure 2: ii) generates sensations of *intense fear and generalized anxiety*.[42] These subjective qualia are accompanied by the somatic concomitants of anxiety (discussed in the text above) and by "arrest" reactions and "flight" behaviours. Similar reactions are obtained from stimulation of the afferent and efferent connections of basolateral amygdala.
- Stimulation of the medial parts of the amygdaloid complex (cortical and central nuclei: Figure 2: iii) generates sensations of *anger and rage*. These qualia are accompanied by the somatic concomitants of aggression and by "fight" behaviours (such as baring of teeth, growling, hissing, piloerection, etc.). Similar reactions are obtained from stimulation of the afferent and efferent connections of cortical and central amygdala.[43]

Stimulation of secondary and tertiary limbic zones (defined above) generates more complex emotions and associated somatic changes. However, due to the very dense interdigitation of corticoid, allocortical, and paralimbic structures, it is not easy to distinguish simple and complex affects at different levels of the limbic system. It is nevertheless possible to identify interconnected circuits within the limbic system—or "spheres of influence" (Panksepp, 1985)—

[41] The centres producing these effects are primarily cholinergic (cf. fns 2 and 31). They also contain abundant opioid receptors.

[42] The quality of anxiety generated by basolateral amygdaloid stimulation is of a fearful (generalized) type. This type of anxiety responds to benzodiazepines (acting on GABA receptors) but not to opiates or to antidepressants. Fear-anxiety is distinguished from panic-anxiety (discussed below). The latter type of anxiety responds to antidepressants (acting on noradrenergic receptors) and to some opiates, but not to benzodiazepines.

[43] These circuits, too, are cholinergic. Anticholinergics are effective anti-aggressive agents (cf. fns 2, 31). Sex hormones also control activity in these circuits; testosterone, in particular, uniformly promotes aggressiveness. There is evidence to suggest that this "rage" circuit of the brain operates in a reciprocal relationship with the "pleasure-lust" centres discussed above (cf. fn. 41). See Panksepp (1998) for a detailed review of these basic-emotion command systems.

which are associated with different affects. These overlapping circuits include all three grades of limbic cortex as well as the subcortical limbic nuclei. I shall now describe three examples of this complex type.

- Stimulation of (paralimbic) orbitofrontal cortex (Figure 2: iv) generates complex feelings of *interest and curiosity*. These feelings are accompanied by somatic appetitive changes (salivation, etc.) and by active engagement with objects in the outside world ("approach" behaviour). Similar reactions are obtained from stimulation of afferent and efferent connections of orbitofrontal cortex.[44]
- Stimulation of the (paralimbic) cingulate gyrus (Figure 2: v) generates feelings of *panic and sorrow*. These feelings are accompanied by somatic concomitants of anxiety and by "attachment" behaviour (i.e. behaviours associated with separation distress, but also by grooming and vocalization). Similar reactions are obtained from stimulation of afferent and efferent connections of the cingulate gyrus.[45]
- Stimulation of the (allocortical) hippocampus (Figure 2: vi) generates *generalized anxiety, episodic reminiscences, and feelings of familiarity*. These feelings[46] are sometimes accompanied by

[44] These circuits are dopaminergic. Antipsychotics (which control the positive symptoms of schizophrenia and some forms of mania) inhibit activity in these circuits. Catecholaminergic stimulants (e.g. antidepressants, amphetamines) activate these circuits (cf. fns 2 and 31). Accordingly, these "interest-curiosity" circuits overlap both anatomically and chemically with "pleasure-lust" centres (cf. fn. 41 above). They appear to generate the *expectation* of pleasure. I have elsewhere (Solms, 1997a, 2000) discussed in detail the fundamental role these circuits play in the generation of dreams.

[45] Panic attacks are associated with object loss or the *anticipation* of object loss. This type of anxiety responds to antidepressants (acting on noradrenergic receptors) and to some opiates, but not to benzodiazepines (cf. fn. 42 above).

[46] Episodic memory and feelings of familiarity may be described as complex emotions for the reason that they represent internalized states in the form of subjective experiences. These complex experiences *represent* unconscious memory traces (i.e. traces of previous external perceptions) *combined with* feelings of subjective presence (i.e. interal perception of the self) as complex internal perceptions; the reminiscences are not the memory traces themselves. Neuropsychological studies have demonstrated conclusively that long-term

> somatic concomitants of anxiety and by "orientation" and "arrest" reflexes (but not by active engagement with objects). Similar reactions are obtained from stimulation of the afferent and efferent connections of the hippocampal formation.[47]

Considered as a whole, these data suggest that the physiological correlates of affect are (to a certain extent) represented topographically. However, *whereas the perceptual zones of externally oriented cortex responded to discrete neurochemical impulses at highly specific locations, the perceptual zones of internally oriented cortex respond to "unbound"*[48] *neurochemical and hormonal changes that spread across diffuse, overlapping fields*. These overlapping fields represent chemical and humoral "spheres of influence".[49] Thus "state-dependent" changes (which represent the changing state of the living organism) generate different affective qualities at different limbic locations. This is the topographic basis of internal perceptual qualia.

That concludes my overview of the physical correlates of affect. It is possible to provide a far more comprehensive account of the anatomy and physiology of affect than of its metapsychology. This is due to the previously mentioned directional bias of the mental apparatus (footnote 17). As a result of this bias, internal conscious-

---

memory traces remain essentially intact following limbic–cortical lesions (Jacoby, 1984). However, *conscious* reminiscence (subjective, episodic memory) is severely disrupted.

Freud (1950 [1895]) equated long-term memory traces with alterations in the "contact barriers" (i.e. synapses) connecting the "ψ nucleus" with the "ψ pallium". These traces became the "mnemic systems" of the *Ucs.* (1900a), which were later subsumed into the unconscious portion of the structural ego (1923b).

I have elsewhere (Solms, 1995) described some of the very complex emotional syndromes that arise from damage to the memory traces themselves. These syndromes are caused by direct damage to the thing-presentations underlying the body image (cf. Damasio, 1994).

[47] These circuits are probably cholinergic. Acetylcholine sourced in the basal forebrain (sexual pleasure) area activates episodic memory circuits (cf. fns 2 and 31).

[48] I have discussed the neurophysiological correlates of the process of "binding" elsewhere (Kaplan-Solms & Solms, 2000).

[49] Cf. Freud's remark that "endogenous stimuli consist of chemical products, *of which there may be a considerable number*" (1950 [1895], p. 321; emphasis added).

ness is experienced in discontinuous sequences, and its contents are highly elusive. External consciousness, by contrast, is subjectively continuous, and its contents are relatively stable. For these reasons, it is possible to perceive material events as a more-or-less complete sequence.[50] The material sequence includes processes that are correlated with unconscious portions of the psychic sequence. This inequality between material and psychic perception provides us with unique opportunities to test our metapsychological inferences against empirical data (i.e. against complete and stable perceptual material). However, this can only be done by means of original research that is undertaken specifically for that purpose (cf. Kaplan-Solms & Solms, 2000; Solms, 1997a).

I will have achieved the goals that I set for this chapter if I have convinced the reader of the principle that systematic research into the unconscious determinants of affect using the methods of physical science is both conceptually legitimate and practically feasible. I trust that I have also said enough about current neuroscientific knowledge to demonstrate that the available physical data are *broadly consistent* with Freud's metapsychological formulations, which were derived from psychic data.[51] At the least, I hope the reader will agree that there are abundant points of contact between modern neuroscientific data and our classical metapsychological model. These points of contact provide rich opportunities for future research, which might start from the observation that *a unitary physiological and anatomical system (the limbic system) centrally regulates vegetative processes, endogenous drives, instinctual behaviours, personal reminiscences, and emotional feelings simultaneously*. This suggests that these superficially diverse functions share a common underlying mechanism—which is what the classical Freudian affect theory predicts.

---

[50] I am referring here to visual perception in particular. Specifically, in the case of the body, I am referring to "anatomical preparations" (i.e. to scientific observation), not to subjective somatic sensations.

[51] Assertions to the contrary by Amacher (1965, 1974), Holt (1965), McCarley & Hobson (1977), and Hadley (1992) are based on serious misunderstandings of the conceptual status of metapsychology (see Solms, 1997d).

Clinical implications

I will conclude this chapter with some brief and tangential remarks on the clinical implications of my conceptualization of affect. The conceptualization I have presented is most obviously pertinent to the treatment of psychosomatic conditions, where we need to find a way of understanding how a bodily symptom—or a physical disease—occurs at a point where an emotional feeling was called for. In cases such as these, the unequal access of unconscious processes to the physical and psychic surfaces of consciousness is sometimes a matter of urgent concern. Similar problems arise in the psychoanalytic treatment of patients who are, for one or another reason, taking psychiatric medication. In these cases it is helpful to have a coherent metapsychological understanding of the influence that the drugs exert upon the mind. The same is true (although perhaps to a lesser degree) when treating certain forms of addiction. I have already referred to psychotic states of projection in which the patient confuses his internal (psychic) perceptions with external (physical) objects. This confusion between the two classes of perception reaches its most extreme form in the "organ speech" of the schizophrenic, whereby internally generated feelings are confused with the internal organs of the body.

The conceptualization I have presented is also relevant to our understanding of the psychoanalytic process in general. I said at the outset that the whole of psychoanalysis is predicated upon particular assumptions about the relationship between the mind and the body. If it is true that the unconscious reality within us is consciously represented in two primary perceptual forms, the one being emotional feelings and the other being the sensations arising from the physical body, then it is entirely consistent with this (and with the fundamental aims of psychoanalysis) that we should relate our deepest interpretations to these two primary things. The surest route to perceptual awareness of an internal reality (an "unconscious phantasy" in the Kleinian sense) will be through an interpretation that links the patient's *emotional state* with his *experience of his physical body*. This is the precise point at which psychic reality confronts external reality (and therefore where the pleasure principle meets the reality principle). If the aim of psychoanalysis is to assist the ego in its impossible task of mediating between the contradictory demands of the drives and reality, then an integration of the emotional ego with the bodily ego would surely be a central goal of psychoanalytic treatment.[52] Such integration (which can only be achieved through the linking function of language) brings to the conscious surface the real (unconscious) unity that exists between mind and body.

But if one follows the historical development of the Freudian tradition in psychoanalysis, from Freud's first observations on the curious symptomatology of hysteria and neurasthenia right up to the present day, then one will find that these psychoanalysts have always linked patients' emotional states with their experience of their bodies. The following quotation from a contribution to a recent symposium on interpretation testifies to the continued vitality of that core tradition:

> In order to locate the source of *anxiety* in a way that makes it meaningful to the patient . . . we have to include the patient's relationship to his or her *physical body* in our thinking. . . . The patient's experience of the external world and of the analyst and the anxiety he experiences in these relationships has to be able to contain his past and present relationship to his own body, if experience and external reality is [to be] invested with meaning. [Laufer, 1994, p. 1098; emphasis added]

The same author warns us to be alert to those psychopathological states in which conscious references to emotions or the sexual body (or to both) are conspicuous by their absence.

I will conclude by adding a brief remark on countertransference (in the British sense of the word, which comes close to meaning "empathy"—Heimann, 1950). The mind of the analyst is, of course, constructed according to the same basic plan as that of the patient. The analyst, too, therefore, can only perceive affects on the

---

[52] Damasio (1994, 1999) has made the interesting suggestion that affect—which he conceptualizes as a representation of the state of the body—is the subjective point of reference for our external perceptual experiences. This, he points out, solves the "binding problem" that has so beset contemporary cognitive science (cf. Dennett, 1991). In this he seems to have re-discovered—from a different point of view—Freud's (1923b, p. 26) famous axiom to the effect that "the ego is first and foremost a bodily ego".

internal surface of consciousness. An emotion can never be registered, as such, on the external surface of the mind. This simple consequence of the design of the mental apparatus helps us to make sense of the otherwise problematic fact that we register the current state of our *patient's* internal world by looking *inwards*, and by thereby exposing ourselves to the feelings that arise from within *ourselves* (see footnote 7). In this respect, too, which borders on the parapsychological, affect may be described as a "sixth sense".

CHAPTER THREE

Mode of operation of unconscious mental processes as revealed by pathological forms of cognition

Thomas Freeman

The forms that thinking, perceiving, and remembering assume under the conditions of mental pathology provide a glimpse of a mode of mental functioning that occasionally plays a part in the mental life of the healthy. Pathological forms of cognition take the place of goal-directed, abstract thinking and a veridical representation of reality. Aberrant forms of cognition are a feature of the functional psychoses (the schizophrenias, maniacal psychoses) and organic mental states. Thinking, perceiving, and remembering are disorganized. Through a detailed study conducted over some time, it becomes possible to identify the action of the unconscious mental processes that lead to pathological forms of cognition.

Pathological forms of thinking as substitutes for rational thought

Verbal communication with patients suffering from non-remitting schizophrenias and organic mental states is impeded by perseveration (Freeman, 1969; Schilder, 1953). Utterances are repeated automatically. They continue despite the patient's attention being drawn to another subject. Perseveration is usually associated with pathological thought content. There is also a lack of grammatical construction. Nouns, verbs, and conjunctions are omitted. In the case of the non-remitting schizophrenias, this disorder of thinking may be preceded or followed by utterances that occur in the colloquial and vernacular speech of the mentally healthy. An individual may describe another by a single perceived characteristic. The following is an utterance of a male schizophrenic patient who said: "See that nurse—that's a 'for Christ's sake' nurse." What he could not say was: "He (the nurse) is always shouting 'for Christ's sake'."

When thinking is disordered, forms of thought that present the idea of similarity between the self and another appear.

> Instead of saying "I am as handsome as the portrait in the Art Gallery", a schizophrenic patient said: "I was a perfect Art Gallery face." When in a dejected mood, the same man complained: "I am the Hunchback of Notre Dame." This means of describing similarity may also occur in the context of abstract ideas. Another patient, usually withdrawn, shouted: "I am history." Knowledge of this man's delusional reality indicated that what he wanted to say was: "I am an historical personage of great importance—namely Charles Edward Stuart, the Young Pretender."

These schizophrenic patients use the same means to represent a perceived similarity between two persons.

> A female patient who knew the writer well greeted him as follows: "I was thinking you must be a commercial traveller when I saw your briefcase; travellers used to come into the shop." This verbal utterance was her means of expressing a

critical transference thought: "You are the same as the commercial travellers who come to sell their wares—I see through you."

Characteristic of the thinking disorder in these schizophrenias of the hebephrenic–catatonic type is the inappropriate use of words. The looseness of the connection between the word (the sign) and the idea or object it is meant to represent (the signified) results in phrases and sentences becoming substitutes for other phrases and sentences. The following is drawn from group sessions with schizophrenic patients (Freeman, Cameron, & McGhie, 1958).

> A silent male patient was pressed by the two psychiatrists in the group to respond to a question put to him. Another patient took out a pencil and a piece of paper. He made a quick sketch. Asked what it was, he replied: "It's two bears; they are trying to lower a blind man down a well and drink at the bottom." This patient was ridiculing the psychiatrists for their puny efforts. On another occasion, a patient, this time a woman, said—"I was afraid of the two umbrellas in case their handles damaged me, so I stayed out in the rain. Now I can shelter under the two umbrellas" (a positive thought). As it was winter, the two psychiatrists taking the group sessions had brought their umbrellas into the group room. Both patients could only express their thoughts in substitutive form.

Substitution of words for other words occurs in cases of chronic brain syndrome.

> An elderly patient could not recall the writer's occupation. He had a short-term memory defect. In past years he had been a motor mechanic and believed he was still working with cars. When asked again about the writer's occupation, he answered—"Aren't you for repairing machines?" The substitute word is usually chosen from some current impression. This was so in this instance (machine = brain = psychiatrist). When another patient was asked to name a watch, the choice of word was determined by the writer's pipe and matches on the table. Instead of saying "It's a watch", he said: "It's a thing I never

> used in my life . . . plenty watches. . . . I didn't need them—used to use it all my life . . . tobacco, pipe, matches, I didn't use them—never used them, stopped altogether." The perseverative trend led to his calling an ashtray a "gas pipe" and keys "pipe and time clocks".

As in the examples cited, substitutions can give representation to wish and other delusional contents.

> An instance of this is the case of a nurse aged 21. She demonstrated the pathological egocentrism that is characteristic of acute psychotic attacks. Everything she perceived had a self-reference. She said she was going to be married. This was a wish. Her proposed marriage was being delayed and obstructed by persecutors. They had desexualized her by means of electricity emanating from machines in the operating theatres. This young woman's speech was slow. She rarely kept to the subject in hand, her thoughts wandering along apparently irrelevant lines. On one occasion she interposed the name "Largactil" amidst her meandering. There was no apparent reason for this, even though she was being treated with this drug. From time to time the writer made notes in full view on the patient. When asked what brought the name "Largactil" to mind, she replied as follows: "'Larg' is for the three R's: reading, writing and arithmetic. 'Act' is for putting on an act, and 'til' is for the till in the hospital canteen." She added: "A woman looked at me this morning in the canteen in a funny way. I did not like it." She agreed that she was troubled by the writer taking notes. Then she went on to say: "You are putting on an act for my benefit." She was unsure of my motives and those of the other doctors who came into the ward.
>
> She had the idea that the ward was organized to suggest a ship. The number of beds in the ward was the same as the number of letters comprising the name of a shipping line. One doctor was going to train her to be a ship's nurse. Then she could go to the Far East, where her father lived. When she got there she was to be married to a ship's captain. This example illustrates again how substitutes (Largactil) can provide the means of represent-

ing numerous trains of thought that, given the conditions of healthy mental life, would find expression in correct syntax.

The wishful delusions of the chronic schizophrenias are the expression of a cognition that is of an elementary, pre-logical kind. Phantasy ambitions fulfilled are the rule in male patients, while erotic phantasies occur more often in women. The patients believe that enemies are responsible for their being thwarted. The fact that these delusions have such a specific content—that is, the reversal of the patient's real circumstances—suggests that it is the way in which the word "no" can be expressed. The patient is unable to think and say "No, I'm not ill". For such a thought to find syntactically correct verbal representation would be tantamount to acknowledging the fact of illness. Here the delusions have a defensive aim. It is not only in the schizophrenias that "no" is represented by reversal. Reversal of an unacceptable reality is the rule in chronic brain syndrome. Hospitalized patients insist that they are at home, busily engaged in their work, as when they were young.

Perceptual anomalies in the schizophrenias and organic mental states

Loss of perceptual constancy is commonplace in the schizophrenias and organic mental states (Davie & Freeman, 1961). Patients perceive changes in the shape of their own bodies and in the bodies of others. These changes often have an affective basis, as in the case of the schizophrenic man who said: "Miss X has got smaller to respect her father." Perceptual modalities are no longer differentiated, leading to synaesthetic types of phenomena. A patient told a colleague: "A movement in front of my eyes is like hearing a sound in my ears" (Chapman, Freeman, & McGhie, 1959). A female patient announced from time to time that she was having coitus with a voice and with a gramophone record. The voice and music were fused with genital sensations (Davie & Freeman, 1961).

Most striking is the manner in which many patients suffering from schizophrenic psychoses and organic mental states perceive the mental and physical aspects of themselves in others and mental and physical aspects of others in themselves. This is the phenomenon of transitivism (Bleuler, 1911), pointing to the loss of the boundary that differentiates the self from others. The subjective experience may be distressing, as in the case of the female patient who complained that: "She (the persecutor) is cursing me with my voice" or accepted, as in maniacal states where the transitivism expresses a wish-fulfilled: "You are the same as me"—for example, "Your hair is fair", despite the other's hair being black. That transitivism occurs independently of affect (wishes, anxiety) is demonstrated by cases of chronic brain syndrome—for example, the elderly patient who insisted that the writer was a motor mechanic like himself. This fact suggests that transitivism arises initially as a result of psychic dissolution alone and only secondarily becomes involved in mental conflict. The syncretic trend (Werner, 1957) as shown in transitivism finds expression, as earlier examples illustrate, in aberrant concept formation (Schilder, 1953).

Disturbances of memory

On the schizophrenias, Rapaport's (1951) statement is clear and unequivocal: "The criterion of memory disorder is not whether there is retention but whether retained memories are available when necessary and appropriate" (p. 121). In this he follows Bleuler (1911): "Memory as such does not suffer in this disorder. Patients reproduce experiences they had before and after the onset of the illness as well as any normal person . . ." (p. 61). It is in the temporal sequence of experiences recalled and their appropriateness to the present situation that the distortions are clearly apparent. Past events are spoken of as if they are occurring in the present. In this there is a similarity with the chronic brain syndrome. However, the schizophrenic patient can under other circumstances show that he can make the distinction between past and current events.

In some cases of chronic schizophrenia, memories of life experiences prior to the illness are no longer available: the amnesia is selective. Patients deny that they are married or insist that their parents are not the real parents. Gaps in the life history as told by the patient are filled by newly created material, which is usually part of the delusional reality.

The means of representation of dream thoughts as prototypes of pathological forms of cognition

As shown, aberrant forms of cognition give representation to logical, syntactically correct trains of thought. The prototypes of the means whereby pathological forms of cognition find representation are provided by the dreams of the mentally healthy and the neurotically afflicted (Freud, 1900a). The analysis of dreams reveals that the verbal ideas (the thoughts) that the dreamer carries into sleep are subject to changes, which Freud described as follows:

> These (the dream thoughts) usually emerge as a complex of thoughts and memories of the most intricate possible structure, with all the attributes of the trains of thought familiar to us in waking life. [Freud, 1900a, pp. 311–312]

He continued:

> When the whole mass of these dream thoughts is brought under the pressure of the dream work, and its elements are turned about, broken into fragments and jammed together almost like pack ice—the question arises of what happens to the logical connections which have hitherto formed its framework. What representation do dreams provide for "if", "because", "just as", "although", "either–or", and all the other conjunctions without which we cannot understand sentences or speeches. [p. 312]

The means by which the dream thoughts find representation in the manifest content of a dream is illustrated by the following:

> A female unmarried patient in psychoanalytic treatment dreamt: "*A female colleague who has two daughters and a two-year-old son has been abandoned by her husband*." The patient's associations were as follows—the female colleague has *two* daughters but no son. The colleague's name is Kay. She added that she has another female colleague who has *two* daughters and a two-year-old son. This colleague was not in the dream. On the dream day she admired a quilted coat the colleague in the dream was wearing. The patient needs a new coat, and on the evening of the dream she was looking at an advertisement for a quilted coat in a catalogue from a Mail Order firm called *Kay*. That same evening a friend told her that a man the patient "fancied" had abandoned his girlfriend. She had the idea she could have him if she wanted to. She said she had a poor opinion of her colleagues' husbands. They were probably impotent.

Numerous trains of thought lay within the manifest content of the dream. The immediate stimulus was the wish to have a new quilted coat like her colleague's. This was carried into the dream. "The nature of the psychic material out of which dreams are made" (Freud, 1900a), was such as to represent that wish and others in its own idiosyncratic fashion—that is, no longer in accord with the rules of syntax. Different dream thoughts contradicted one another. The thought "I wish I was married, like my colleague" found expression. Through identification she became the same as they were. There was the contradictory thought: "I am not envious of them *because* their husbands are impotent." This negative, or "No", could only find representation through a reversal of content: "I have not been left by a man, someone else has." In fact, a man friend had broken off a relationship with her some months earlier. This sense of being abandoned could be traced to her belief that in childhood she was neglected by her mother in favour of her two younger sisters, who were now married.

The same means of representation are to be found in schizophrenic patients during the acute and chronic stages of the illness. The wish to be identical to another person and possess all that he/she has is illustrated in the following.

> A chronically ill female schizophrenic patient (Miss A) was being seen daily in her ward in the hope of establishing a psychotherapeutic relationship. One day the psychiatrist who was treating her stopped to talk to another patient named Alford. He spent some time conversing with her in full view of Miss A. When he came to see Miss A the following day, she was silent and no longer friendly in manner as she had been. "Why are you so quiet, Miss A", he asked. She turned to him angrily, shouting: "My name is Alford." During his following visits, Miss A continued to insist that her name was Alford. Through identification, the patient was saying: "No, I'm not Miss A, I'm Miss Alford" (transference).

Freud's (1900a) concept of composition describes the situation where the dream image consists of features belonging to one or more of the individuals in the latent dream thoughts. Composition can be observed in the content of the utterances of schizophrenic patients.

> A well-educated schizophrenic woman accused the psychiatrist, with whom she had regular sessions, of being a wizard: "Come over here and bring your lump of magic with you", she said to him. She accused him of casting a spell over her and playing tricks with her. She threatened to kill him with a magic bullet. Familiar with Scottish myth and history, the psychiatrist recognized that the patient believed him to be the Jacobite leader, Graham of Claverhouse, whose enemies had claimed that he was a wizard. He had been killed with a silver bullet—the traditional means of killing magicians.

The creation of the composite figure of psychiatrist and Claverhouse replaced the sexual wish phantasy (transference) that had been awakened through the ongoing psychotherapeutic contact. A persecutory delusion was the outcome. If this had been the dream of a neurotic patient, the psychiatrist would have appeared as a wizard in the manifest content of the dream with all the details described by the schizophrenic patient.

These clinical examples illustrate the similarities that exist between the way in which logical trains of thought are represented by patients suffering from schizophrenic psychoses and in the dreams of the mentally healthy. In both there is the loss of an advanced mental function. A less advanced form of cognition takes the place of correct syntax. The pathological forms of thought are thus positive symptoms in the Jacksonian sense (Jackson, 1884).

Pathological forms of cognition and unconscious mental processes

Describing the cognitive processes and their disturbances separately, as in the present chapter, detracts from the fact that they act in concert and in a unified manner. Rapaport's (1951) concept of cognitive organizations provides a realistic way of envisaging the operation of cognitive processes. The waking state of attention, day dreaming, the hypnagogic state, dreams, and psychoses are characterized by different types of cognitive organization.

The examples of mental pathology that have been described depict similar changes occurring over the whole range of the cognitive functions—that is, affecting the totality of the cognitive organization. There is syncretism (Werner, 1957) and an ease of creation of substitutes in thinking, perceiving, and remembering. Transitivism reflects the syncretism in the sphere of interpersonal relations; verbal ideas are fused with other ideas, leading to over-inclusive thinking and aberrant concept formation (Payne, 1961; Schilder, 1953); perceptual modalities are no longer differentiated with the appearance of synaesthetic phenomena; past and recent memory schemata become confused. It is through substitution that pathological forms of cognition replace ordered conceptual thinking, which follows the rules of syntax. That the cognitive organization that characterizes the schizophrenias is subject to the influence of affects is shown by the changes that take place in that organization either in the direction of increased pathology or towards a cognition attuned to reality.

The similarities that exist between the dreams of the mentally healthy and the pathological cognition of the schizophrenias is not confined to the means of representation, which themselves reflect the status of the respective cognitive organizations. Syncretism and the formation of substitutes are paramount. Syncretism, in the sphere of thinking, was described by Freud (1900a) as "condensation". Condensation "products" arise on the basis of elements common to different trains of thought, as in the instances of the nurse who said "Largactil" and the dream of the patient in which the number *two* and the name *Kay* were prominent. Condensation stands in contrast to the differentiated mental processes that characterize the cognitive organization of the state of consciousness that underpins the capacity to attend and concentrate. Substitutes are formed from the displacement of emphasis from one idea or group of ideas to another idea or group of ideas. In conjunction with the archaic (pre-logical) means of representation, condensation and displacement (Freud's primary process, 1900a) are responsible for the formation of the manifest content of a dream and the pathological form of thinking, perceiving, and remembering. These phenomena reveal the action of mental processes that are in themselves unconscious.

In the dreams of the mentally healthy and in forms of pathological cognition the reversion (formal regression, Freud, 1900a) to archaic types of cognitive organization is a primary event caused by the psychic dissolution that attends sleep and states of mental pathology. Organic mental states illustrate this in a most striking fashion. When there is a clash between wish phantasies, ethical standards, and the sense of self-esteem, the presence of archaic (pre-logical) forms of thought allows the unacceptable wish phantasies to assume a disguise. This prevents the individual from recognizing the underlying significance of his thinking. Such a conflict is not the cause of the appearance of the cognitive organization of the dream state or of pathological forms of cognition. These organizations have the primary process as their basis. They are not to be confused with the censorship, as in dreams, or the defence, as in abnormal mental states (Freud, 1900a). It follows that not every dream image or aberrant concept is the result of a defence against unacceptable wish phantasies.

Pathological forms of cognition and the dreams of the healthy and neurotically afflicted reveal the mode of action of unconscious mental processes—that is, the primary process. The phenomena that reflect the action of the primary process (Freud, 1900a) offer nothing on the nature of unconscious mental processes themselves.

He writes: "The unconscious is the true psychical reality; in its innermost nature it is as much unknown to us as the reality of the external world by the communications of our sense organs" (p. 613).

In this chapter I have tried to confine myself, as far as possible, to the empirical data and to avoid the temptation to theorize. Thus I have made no reference to Freud's (1900a) theory of mobile cathexes, which he hypothesizes as underlying the action of displacement and condensation (primary process). Equally, I have made no reference to other theories that claim to explain how pathological forms of cognition come to pass.

CHAPTER FOUR

Reflections on the psychoanalytic study of character

Clifford Yorke

> "My dear Tony," she then blandly replied. "I've never known any one like you for not having two grains of observation. I've known people with only a little; but a little's a poor affair. You've absolutely none at all, and that, for your character, is the right thing: it's magnificent and perfect."
>
> Henry James, *The Other House* (1948, pp. 53–54)

A background to reflections

I propose to take, as a background to these few reflections, a selective account, interspersed with comment, of an International Colloquium on Character, held at the Anna Freud Centre in 1990.[1] There have been other international discussions on the psychoanalytic understanding of character, but this was the only one of which I have first-hand knowledge. It was also well

[1] The Twelfth International Colloquium was held at the Anna Freud Centre, London, on 26 and 27 October 1990. Its subject was *Maturational and Experiential Components in Character Formation*.

reported; it covered a good deal of ground; and it raised significant questions, not all of which are in sight of resolution.

Summarizing the proceedings at the closing plenary session, Wallerstein (1991) took the opportunity to state some views of his own. He felt that, while it was helpful and informative, the conference had drawn attention to the *limitations* of psychoanalysis; and the weekend's deliberations had opened up "vast areas of psychoanalytic ignorance" (p. 249). And he added:

> It does suggest that we should look at developments in other areas, in cognate areas, child development, baby watching, cognitive psychology, and all the modelling arising from that; genetic studies, twin studies, epidemiological studies, as well as the biological studies. The data may not be reachable by our methods. . . . [pp. 249–250]

Wallerstein rightly reflected the air of dissatisfaction and uneasiness sometimes evident during the discussion. I doubt that anyone present would have disagreed with the view that psychoanalysis has no *comprehensive* theory of character, as Schlesinger (1991) reminded the gathering at the start of proceedings, recalling the opinions of Abend (1983) and Baudry (1983). That is not to deny that psychoanalysis has contributed a great deal to our understanding of certain character traits and constellations. Most analytic work involves some analysis of maladaptive character traits, generally following the principle that the patient must first become dissatisfied with them (cf. Reich, 1928; Waelder, 1937). A patient who is too comfortable with them to be susceptible to influence, even by the most skilled interventions, is unlikely ever to give them up.[2] And although *character neuroses—neurotic* disorders of character—were barely mentioned at the colloquium, these disturbances have a great deal in common with the *symptom* neuroses and sometimes respond to psychoanalysis. They require cautious assessment: Yorke, Wiseberg, and Freeman (1989) felt that many definitions, even by such careful writers as Waelder (1960) and Baudry (1984), were less than satisfactory, and they attempted

[2] A woman applied for treatment with a character trait as her main concern: "I'm a bitch", she said, "and I don't like it". It was possible to help her.

what they regarded as a more accurate delineation, with clinical examples.[3]

Wallerstein's belief that psychoanalysts should also look to other disciplines in trying to understand character is unlikely to be contested. It is fair to add that analysts have always accepted the importance of heredity, and Freud (e.g. 1905d) repeatedly emphasized it. Psychoanalysts have also contributed to twin studies, and the literature is extensive: papers by Burlingham (1952, 1963) and Abrams (1986) are but examples, though of considerable interest. "Baby watching" has produced valuable information, but it has also led to some questionable psychological theories, and its application to psychoanalytic practice should be looked upon with caution (Yorke, 1995). To name but one cause for care: development does not occur in linear fashion, but is subject to discontinuities as well as continuities, a point applicable to character formation, too, as Abrams emphasized in the course of the colloquium (see below). A patient may regress on the couch, but early infancy will never be replicated in the form in which it occurred in reality.

Psychoanalysts have often felt uncomfortable about the way character can be understood in terms of their own discipline. There is, in any case, a preliminary hurdle to cross in any consideration of the topic: it is essential that psychoanalysts know what they mean by "character" before they can decide how much their discipline can contribute to its psychological understanding. Schlesinger (1991), in his opening address to the same meeting, pointed out that "character" is not in itself a psychoanalytic term, and in everyday usage it has a number of meanings, not all of which are unacceptable to psychoanalysts. Of these, he considered at some length the understanding of character as an enduring aspect of personality. But the term is sometimes used in a negative way by the analyst who feels "he has come to the end of his re-

[3] Here, the briefest summary must suffice. As in the symptom neuroses, fixation points are prominent, but neither regression nor dissolution plays an essential part. The oedipal phase differs from that of symptom neuroses in its form of resolution. "Character neuroses involve a mutual accommodation of id and ego of a different order from that of the symptom neuroses, so that compromise formations are more readily acceptable to their possessor" (p. 217). For a full account, see Yorke, Wiseberg, & Freeman (1989), pp. 70–89.

sources" and "invokes 'character' to account for the obdurateness of resistance, to explain why hoped-for developments have not occurred: that both parties encounter persistent, if not permanent, aspects of personality" (p. 156).

On the other hand, Schlesinger was quite emphatic that there was a positive side to enduring aspects of the personality:

> We hold certain persons in great respect, even awe, just because their characters remain firm, so that they can prevail under the most adverse circumstances. In short, character is an indispensable term for acknowledging that while man is infinitely adaptable, and well equipped to survive, he has (or ought to have) certain relatively immovable internal commitments, a hierarchy of goals and purposes, and a range of permissible and efficient modes of achieving them. These qualities permit others to predict his behaviour, that is to count on his response in a wide range of circumstances. [Schlesinger, 1991, p. 156]

Later, after Duncan McLean had read a summary of his paper (published in full in 1992), which also considered character (*inter alia*) as something existing over time, and the first plenary discussion was underway, doubts about the meaning, and even the usefulness, of character as a concept in psychoanalysis quickly surfaced. Thus, Solnit declared that, in the discussion, the term "character" was beginning to cover a multitude of characteristics. He (a little facetiously) interpreted a previous contribution as suggesting that it would be better never to use the word "character" in talking about it, but to say "what you meant about what you know and what you don't know" (1990, p. 180). And Shengold (1991a, p. 183) shared Solnit's unease and asserted that "what should really come through in the course of this weekend's meeting is how much we do not know about our topic. Human events are infinitely complex and when we try to grasp them for theory-making and heuristic purposes, we have to simplify and over-simplify."

That view is bound to attract sympathy. But it is of interest that Valenstein had, in the meantime, recalled a panel in New York in 1957, chaired by Helen Tartakoff, on the "Psychoanalytic Concept of Character" on which he had reported (Valenstein, 1958). Tartakoff (1966) had said that the original psychoanalytic concept of the basic role played by the drives and their vicissitudes in character formation had neither been outmoded nor substantially revised. Our understanding had been widened: we now gave importance to inborn characteristic ego functions, along with instinctual factors and their interaction, under the influence of early object relations. We were concerned with their subsequent development, in terms of maturation, under the impact of sociocultural influences. To this, Valenstein added:

> By taking on board what Waelder called "The Principle of Multiple Function" (1930 [1936]), the ego must always be seen as responsive functionally within the four co-ordinate agencies, the id, the ego, the superego and reality, and within this system a certain hierarchical organization obtains at any time. [Valenstein, 1991, p. 183]

And he wondered whether it would be possible to devise, perhaps through a digital index,

> a system for typing any particular character, viewed as a relatively fixed or crystallised organisation of specific character traits with respect of these four co-ordinates? [p. 183]

If this is speculative, it seems to me to point in an important direction. By bringing into the debate the relationship of the internal agencies to each other, as well as to the outside world, it points to a possible *metapsychology of character*. For the relationship between *structures* (however stable) is necessarily a *dynamic* one, the strengths and weakness of which are a matter of mental *economics*. This was clearly recognized by Valenstein when he pointed out that we speak of impulsive or "id characters" and obsessional characters with rigid, dominant superegos. And when he referred to a "hierarchical organization that obtains at any time", he must have had in mind the evolutionary and hierarchical concept of mental development that Hughlings Jackson[4] so vigorously asserted and Freud embraced with such enthusiasm.

---

[4] Concerning the nervous system generally, see Jackson, 1884; on mental disorder, see Jackson, 1894. Hughlings Jackson's interest in psychological matters is well attested (e.g. Jackson, 1887).

Freud and character

Valenstein's comments bear closely on the question of Freud's own contributions to the psychoanalytic study of character. These were not ignored at the meeting: Schlesinger (1991) had referred to a number of them, particularly in relation to the Oedipus complex and the superego. McLean (1992) mentioned the early typologies, including Freud's, and pointed to their limitations. There were other references to particular points that Freud had made, and Wallerstein mentioned several in his closing address. But there was no general recognition of the breadth and extent of Freud's contributions *when viewed in the light of his own sweeping theoretical developments.* It may be that all this was taken for granted, and it was thought essential to concentrate on the many contributions made subsequently. I have my doubts, for Freud never brought together his contributions to the psychoanalytic understanding of character in a single unifying paper. That is also true of his theory of affect, as Solms and Nersessian (1999) have pointed out in the process of making good the deficit. Baudry (1983) rendered a sterling service to psychoanalysis when he undertook the task of tracing the evolution of Freud's concept of character. His paper was mentioned by Schlesinger in passing, but not discussed—possibly again because knowledge of it was taken for granted. But when it comes to Freud nowadays, I doubt whether a comprehensive understanding of his work *can* be taken for granted, though it must be emphasized that, at this particular meeting, many of the speakers were Freud experts of high repute.

Baudry's paper repays close attention: it concluded with a useful summary that gathers together the main steps in Freud's developing theory, and it is convenient to paraphrase it here in condensed form and with only minor clarifications for the benefit of those unacquainted with the complete paper. The successive stages are:

1. In Freud's early writings there is no distinct psychoanalytic meaning attached to the term "character".
2. In the *Three Essays,* Freud (1905d) discussed the transformation of drives through reaction formation and sublimation, thus relating them to character traits.

3. The outline of the anal character (Freud, 1908b) relates its constituent traits to a specific stage of drive organization, including its defensive structures, thus relating it to a *developmental* timetable.
4. Two years later, Freud (1910h), discussed a special type of object choice found in men, linking it with repetitive behaviour derived from the Oedipus complex, and in so doing brought types of object relations into the study of character.
5. In the next significant step Freud (1914g) brought repetitive behaviour (in the form of an unconscious acting out in place of memory) into the study of character.
6. The paper on mourning and melancholia (Freud, 1917e) emphasized the importance of developmental processes of the ego in relation to identification. It was no longer a simple matter of cannibalistic forces (cf. Freud, 1912–13), however important these may have been in the subject his paper addressed.
7. In *The Ego and the Id,* Freud (1923b) discussed the ego as a "precipitate of abandoned object cathexes" and the *history* of these object choices in terms of identifications. Later, Freud took the view that identification was not dependent on abandonment, and the clarifications of the concepts of ego-ideal and superego greatly assisted this understanding (cf. 1933a, p. 91). [Schlesinger (1991) briefly referred to this matter.]
8. Freud's (1920g) introduction of aggression into his drive theory added an important dimension to the study of character.
9. Freud (1937c) discussed character in relation to resistance in analysis, as well as problems in character analysis, and had already (1939a [1934–38]) discussed the important question of trauma and its influence on character.

The above is not an exhaustive list of Freud's contributions to the psychoanalytic study of character. It does not, for example, include his important considerations of sexual identity in relation to character (see below). It is a *summarizing* list, concerned with the *development* of the concept, as Baudry makes plain. Freud repeatedly made passing reference to the question of character in his writings, sometimes simply throwing out points and returning to them at a later date. That, after all, was one of his frequent habits, but not always one that made it easy to follow the development of his ideas. But Baudry demonstrates, with clarity, that Freud brought into his concept of character, often over time, a wide range of complex issues, including: the influence of drive derivatives and representations; the influence on behaviour of unconscious fantasies, particularly of a masturbatory quality linked with the oedipal phase; identifications with parents and other significant figures; the influence of the *resolution* of major complexes—the castration and the oedipal; the importance of constitution; the expression of important defensive mechanisms in mental functioning, such as denial, projection, reaction-formation, and others; positive and negative reactions to trauma; the nature and quality of the superego and its involvement in conflict (or as an ideal giving aims to its possessor); and attempts to deal with the effects on character of neurosis and ego distortion. All this, and more, shows the importance of bearing in mind the *developmental* aspects in the evolution of character, emphasized by Abrams. And if there is some repetition in what I have taken from Baudry, I make no apology. It will serve to counter the reductionist and rather pejorative assertion that Freud's is simply a drive psychology, seriously outdated. With this—unhappily common—view goes the rather arrogant assumption that nowadays psychoanalytic views are far in advance of Freud's, unimpeded by nineteenth-century concepts and cultural handicaps, and that the contemporary psychoanalyst can think so much more clearly than he could about psychological matters. That assumption may often be unconscious, but it is a good example of the ambivalence that Freud, as the analytic father, so much invites (cf. Shengold, 1993). The plain fact is that his accomplishments in regard to character are astonishing. There is much to add to what he has said, and a great deal to add in the future; but that is another matter.

Abrams's approach to definition, normality, and pathology

In the closing plenary discussion at the colloquium, one of the panellists, Sam Abrams (1991), dealt, in a succinct and lucid way, with some of the central problems facing those who seek to understand character and its psychological components more fully. He, too, thought the first problem *was* one of definition, and he considered it an advantage to deal with it descriptively. He took a view, consonant with that expressed by Schlesinger (1991), McLean (1992) and others, that "character is an enduring aspect of a person that abides over time, and that is noted by the impact that it has upon other people or upon tasks or upon principles" (Abrams, 1991, p. 213). If that (more or less) met the demands of the first problem, it at once, said Abrams, led to a second: what is normal and what is pathological character? One could still be descriptive in one's approach to this question—for example, in considering as pathological those traits that consistently hurt the self or others. Or one could say that compelling personality features that made no concessions to flexibility were probably pathological. Yet another approach, more akin to a conceptual one, would be to look upon traits that fostered adaptation as normal, and those that led to maladaptation as pathological: Abrams thought this satisfactory as long as we "carefully distinguished adaptation from mere adjustment" (p. 214).

Abrams reminded his audience of Freud's observation that a patient's character could impede or facilitate psychoanalytic work: consistent and abiding traits that interfered with analysis were pathological. It seemed to Abrams that the notion that such traits could best be observed within the clinical context of analytic resistance was felicitous. But it had limitations: we cannot judge someone's normal or pathological character traits solely in terms of their analytic participation. I would agree with Abrams in this: certain pathological traits may, for a variety of reasons, not appear at all during analysis, and non-pathological traits often go undetected: the patient may not bring to analysis matters that cause him no trouble. I do not believe, in any case, that the analyst sees the "whole" of the patient. But for all the reservations—his own or others'—Abrams thought that Freud's observation had been illustrated in the clinical presentations to the meeting (Herzog, 1991; McLean, 1992).

If, said Abrams, character traits were repetitive, more or less predictable, expressions of behaviour that endured over time, then they underlined *continuities*: they persist through adult life, and when we see them in the adult, we try to understand them retrospectively (that is, in terms of personal history). But we now meet a third difficulty: that of *discontinuities* (a point made earlier in this chapter). Abrams referred to clinical presentations, given at the colloquium, illustrating character traits and showing continuities through childhood into adult life. But we had heard, too, of a radical change of character in *latency*, and had been reminded by Harold Blum (in discussion) that we *expected* to see powerful changes of character traits during *adolescence*. Discontinuities, it was clear, must be acknowledged.

How were these discontinuities to be understood? The short answer would be: *through the developmental process*. I thought Abrams put the point very neatly: in the course of human development there was an "expectable sequence of progressive hierarchical organizations appearing in the form of phases or stages characterized by new forms of thinking, new ways of feeling, new adaptive repertoires—that is, potential changes in traits of character" (Abrams, 1991, p. 215).

I have not attempted to summarize all that Abrams said, but for present purposes prefer to comment only on his foregoing remarks. First, there is the question of definition. In 1984, Baudry put forward the suggestion that character could be understood at two levels: a *clinical* one, which offered data for observation (character *traits*), and a more abstract one (character *organization*). In this, he tried "to describe the unique aspect of character, that is, its capacity to establish a relation between a superficial attribute and a deep structure" (p. 455). And he suggests that "character represents the core of an individual from a particular point of view—a precipitate of a person's relations to the outside world" (p. 455). This view does not invalidate what Abrams said but might help to augment it, providing that *precipitate* is understood to include relations to what was *once* the outside world. The developmental viewpoint is crucial to both. Baudry (1989) later elaborated on his view of character *organization*, though neither paper attracted much attention at the colloquium.

The concept of "enduring" character traits, largely predictable and repetitive, is certainly, for the most part, true of the adult, but it cannot be applied wholesale while character is still developing. That fact is clearly recognized in Abrams's description of the developmental process. For all that, caution is called for: there are many adults whose character traits are, in certain respects, remarkably *unpredictable.*[5] It is true, to say the least, that this borders on the pathological, if not the unquestionably aberrant.

The subject of continuities and discontinuities is a fascinating one. In this regard I will quote from a case history to be found elsewhere, and which will serve some further purposes:

> Ralph was 21 at the time of assessment. A developmental history was available from the mother. He was, according to her, "lazy from the word go." From birth onward it was difficult to keep him awake, and it was a family joke that, in his childhood, wherever he was found, he would be asleep. Even during his feeds it was difficult to keep him awake. In adult life, he would choose fluid or semifluid nourishment in preference to food that needed mastication. He had been a passive boy who had delighted in prolonged mothering; he was still bathed by his mother at the age of 12. In school as in adult life he was devoid of ambition, and never learned to read or write properly, although psychological testing indicated that this was well within his capacity. In his sexual life he was singularly passive, waiting always on the woman's initiative; and his sexual activities were largely prompted by a passive compliance with directions to take part in sex shows for which he was paid. Even then, as in private, he could only undertake active intercourse through the artificial "pep" supplied by methedrine. He never quarrelled, argued, fought, or said "no" to anybody. His passivity was almost complete. The diagnostician felt, understandably, disinclined to recommend a couch for him to lie on. [Yorke, 1983, pp. 390–391]

This highly selective extract from a very detailed case history emphasizes a *continuity* in the form of a prominent, lifelong character trait—passivity. Certainly the case is highly unusual and the trait concerned pronounced to a pathological degree rarely to be encountered. The passivity, at various stages, entered into other pathological phenomena barely touched on here: the drug taking

[5] There is scope for further investigation of unpredictability as a feature of character. It is clearly different from characteristic responses to particular situations, where, for example, someone who is normally agreeable and accommodating responds with considerable anger under certain conditions, only to recover his customary composure when the situation is past.

(which included serious "main-line" heroin addiction) was in line with the passivity but could not be explained on that basis alone.

It is worth adding that this patient had at one point suffered from an amphetamine psychosis. It is well known that this disorder has a remarkably similar presentation in individuals who otherwise differ widely from each other in terms of character. Symptoms include paranoid delusions of similar content; but the symptoms clear up when the use of amphetamine is given up. Suspiciousness and a tendency to experience others as hostile may not have played any part in their psychological make-up in the normal course of their lives; and these features were certainly absent in the patient under discussion. So one adventitious source of personality change (a *discontinuity*) may be brought about by drugs, however temporary that change may be. And we should remember, too, perhaps, that personality change occurs not only in psychotic states but in *physical illness* too. An increase in narcissism in the bodily ill is an everyday occurrence. But it may rightly be said that, following recovery, the individual once more displays his customary, *enduring* character traits, unless the illness was severely traumatizing, and something like a post-traumatic neurotic-like state (see Yorke, 1986) supervened, in which character changes could also be found.

Freud also considered the narcissism of hypochondriasis. Here I will only point to the extreme narcissism of severe *monosymptomatic* hypochondriasis. This condition is refractory to almost any kind of psychological treatment: It is impossible to hold the patient's attention for more than the shortest spell of time, because that interest is virtually exclusively held by the patient's body. Depersonalization may also bring character changes, but the matter needs fuller consideration than can be given here: a number of different conditions are sometimes covered by the same rubric.

The character changes in latency and adolescence have already been mentioned. This may remind us of the role of puberty in relation to these changes. It is well known that pre-adolescence may declare itself in many striking ways: a child who has been reasonably clean, tidy, and obedient may, in pre-adolescence, display these characteristics in reverse. The changes that may occur in adolescence are beyond brief summary, even if that were needed; but we should perhaps remind ourselves that personality changes can also occur in the menopause. If they do, the question arises: are they reversible, or do they endure? And it may also be worth referring to the increased narcissism that is often a feature of old age.[6]

Character and internal conflict

There may be more to be gained by a return to the case so briefly described above. The patient's passivity was not only compounded by the use of heroin (which induces passivity *chemically*): it profoundly affected his sexual life, even before he used that drug. It seems worth recalling that Anna Freud (1962) distinguished three types of conflict. The first was *external* conflict, which is more or less self-explanatory. The second was *internalized* conflict: what had once been external became an independent part of the internal world. The third was *internal* conflict and consisted of inborn tendencies of an opposing nature: active versus passive; masculine versus feminine; and love versus hate. I did not hear internal conflict mentioned as such in the Anna Freud Centre symposium, though it may have been raised in small group discussion.[7] Yet the balance between these opposing forces has a profound effect on character.

There is a difficulty, however, for the diagnostician who is undertaking the psychoanalytic assessment of a potential patient. It is often far from easy, in putting together a profile, to say to what extent these conflicting tendencies are due to *internal* conflict, how far they are affected by *internalized* conflict or, especially in the young, by *external* influences or conflicts. In the patient described above, everything points to the strength of the constitutional factor reflected in the passivity, irrespective of the contributions that may

---

[6] This is beautifully satirized by Wyndham Lewis in the prologue to his novel *The Apes of God* (1930).

[7] However, in the closing summary, Wallerstein (1991, p. 249) referred to a comment by Tony Kris, endorsed by Colette Chiland, about the importance of sexual identity in character formation. Wallerstein said, rightly, that these should have been talked about more generally. I do not recall, however, a discussion of *bisexual conflict* in relation to this issue.

have been made to it at various times. In other cases, matters are far less clear-cut: activity may be used *secondarily* to defend against passivity and vice versa; masculinity against femininity; and so on.

> A girl of 7 was brought for treatment on account of strong wishes to be a boy. She was graceful, charming, friendly, and gifted, but none of these attributes did anything to offset her unhappiness. She said to the diagnostician, with what proved to be a customary simplicity and clarity: "There is something spoiling my life because I want to be a Daddy when I grow up."
>
> She was the third child and first daughter of warmly affectionate parents who shared, in early infancy, her handling and care. By the age of only 10 months, her relationship to her mother was indeed a good one, but was matched by an unusually close attachment to her father. Just before she was 2 years of age, the mother gave birth to a fourth child, a boy, and the girl's closeness to her father became even more pronounced. By the age of three, the closeness was excessive to a point that embarrassed the father, who began to withdraw and went to work in another town. The girl, disturbed by what she saw as parental betrayal in favour of the new boy, abandoned her femininity, and her penis envy was intensified.[8] From that time onward she refused to wear dresses or any kind of feminine clothing, and this refusal persisted right up to her assessment and for some time after treatment started. (For a fuller account, see Yorke, Wiseberg, & Freeman, 1989, pp. 26–28.)

A diagnostic formulation, making use of both history and case material, would suggest that a striking early attachment to the father and growing rejection of the mother furthered an unusually early entry into the oedipal situation, and one incapable of successful mastery. A reversion to the phallic phase allowed some return to closer maternal attachment, with the tie to the father retained through identification. The reader will easily suspect other contributing factors, even from the scanty information given in this

[8] All this would be speculative, were it not for clarification during psychoanalytic treatment.

vignette. But it can safely be said that the child's unhappiness did not arise from *internal* conflicts alone, but was profoundly responsive to external events and to the growing *internalized* conflicts engendered by them.

Indeed, this abbreviated story illustrates the way in which developmental factors can shift the bisexual balance. And a girl's failure to negotiate the oedipal phase does not necessarily result in a strengthened masculinity and a pull towards homosexuality: it may ultimately lead, as Freud insisted on more than one occasion, to the renunciation of a sexual life altogether. (See, however, Edgcumbe & Burgner, 1975, referred to below.)

Internal conflicts do not act entirely independently but may strongly influence each other. A woman with profound masculine tendencies (whether conscious or not) may, at least in some respects, *hate* her *femininity*; but if, in spite of this, she engages in intercourse with a man, she may only be able to reach satisfaction if she sits on top of him and assumes an entirely *active* role. In the case of the man described above, the passivity was reflected in his sexual life: it should be added that the full history was strongly suggestive of deep feminine trends.

Character and sexual identity

It is beyond the scope of the present reflections to delve too deeply into the intricacies of character formation in relation to sexual development and a sense of sexual identity. The subject is riddled with complexities and has fostered a vast literature, much of it controversial. But one or two additions to the foregoing remarks may be made.

First, caution is called for in considering the mutual influences of internal conflicts in the development of masculinity and femininity, and their possible effects on character. Certainly, passivity is not to be *equated* with femininity, or masculinity with activity. It is true that, in adult sexual life, the man normally plays by far the more active part, and a very passive man may view that role with reluctance. Equally, the woman normally enjoys the receptive part she plays. But that receptivity is normally never wholly passive, devoid of all activity. In this connection, it seems worth mentioning a woman who, when a man approached her with the intention of making love, gave herself up to him, the moment she was touched, *with complete flaccidity*. She became entirely limp, as if she were a corpse. That degree of passivity is, of course, both rare and pathological.

In this connection it may be recalled that Freud made the following remarks:

> Psycho-analysis has a common basis with biology, in that it presupposes an original bisexuality in human beings (as in animals). But psycho-analysis cannot elucidate the intrinsic nature of what in biological phraseology is termed "masculine" and "feminine": it simply takes over the two concepts and makes them the foundation of its work. When we attempt to reduce them further, we find masculinity *vanishing* into activity and femininity into passivity, and that does not tell us enough. [Freud, 1920a, p. 171]

The italics are added; the word is crucial. Towards the end of his life, Freud, discussing the different courses followed by boys and girls in traversing the Oedipus complex, stated, quite emphatically:

> We are faced here with the great enigma of the biological fact of the duality of the sexes: it is an ultimate fact for our knowledge, it defies every attempt to trace it back to something else. Psychoanalysis has contributed nothing to clearing up this problem. . . . [Freud, 1940a, p. 188]

And, in terms of mental life, he calls the distinction between the sexes on the basis of activity and masculinity "an inadequate, empirical and conventional equation", adding that the "fact of psychological bisexuality, too, embarrasses all our enquiries into the subject and makes them harder to describe" (p. 188). To speak of passivity or activity in any given individual is, therefore, to refer to the balance struck between the two opposing trends in *either* sex. And the one trend or the other may be more evident in particular circumstances, may be brought into service for defensive purposes, strengthened through identifications, or modified from other sources and for all sorts of reasons. Indeed, Freud pointed out that:

> a mother is active in every sense towards her child; the act of lactation itself may equally be described as the mother suckling the baby or as her being sucked by it. *The farther you go from the sexual sphere the more obvious will the "error of superimposition"*[9] *become.* Women can display great activity in various directions, men are not able to live in company with their own kind unless they develop a large amount of passive adaptability. [Freud, 1933a, p. 115; emphasis added]

And, a little later, he adds:

> One might consider characterizing femininity psychologically as giving preference to passive *aims* [emphasis added]. This is not of course the same thing as passivity; to achieve a passive aim may call for a large amount of activity. It is perhaps the case that in a woman, on the basis of her share of the sexual function, a preference for passive behaviour and passive aims is carried over into her life to a greater or lesser extent, in proportion to the limits, restricted or far-reaching, within which her sex life serves as a model. But we must beware in this of underestimating the influence of social customs, which similarly force women into passive situations.[10] All this is far from being cleared up. [pp. 115–116]

Turning to the conflict between love and hate, it is self-evident that both exist in either sex. That is not, however, the end of the matter: there are links between aggression *as the drive behind hate* and sexual identity, and there are also the different ways of *falling in love*—and perhaps of *loving*—that have links with sexual identity. Let us return to Freud:

> There is one particularly constant relation between femininity and instinctual life which we do not want to overlook. The suppression of women's aggressiveness which is prescribed for them constitutionally and imposed on them socially[11] favours the development of powerful masochistic impulses, which succeed, as we know, in binding erotically the destructive trends which have been diverted inwards. [pp. 115–116]

---

[9] That is, the confusion of two different things with each other.

[10] So much for the common assertion that Freud failed to take social and cultural factors into account in addressing these issues.

[11] Note that in the United States women are now trained to fight in the U.S. Marines.

If masochism were indeed a truly feminine trait, the fact that it is so often met with in men would, Freud suggests, make it obligatory to attribute this aspect of femininity to its masculine possessors. On the other hand we know that sadism (and its reverse, masochism) reaches its height in the anal sadistic phase, and that is as true for girls as it is for boys. Here again, Freud says: "analysis of children's play has shown that the aggressive impulses leave nothing to be desired in the way of abundance and violence". On their entry into the phallic phase, "the little girl is a little man". The differences between sexes are temporarily overshadowed. Reference to the oedipal phase is made below.

Freud (1914c; see also, e.g., 1910h, 1912d, 1918a, and many later works, e.g. 1933a) had a good deal to say about object choice in relation to falling in love. The child's need for feeding, care, and protection brings with it love of the "anaclitic" or "attachment" type (see Strachey's footnote 2 to Freud, 1914c, p. 87, the work to which these remarks refer). In some disturbances, sexual perversions, and types of homosexuality the attachment is not to the mother but to the self, but this kind of narcissistic object choice was assumed to be present in human beings generally, though in different proportions.

The differences between male and female object choice are not found universally. Generally speaking, in the male, object-love is of the attachment type, derived from infantile narcissism *but* transferred to the sexual object so that a sexual overvaluation of the object results. In the female, Freud thought that, with puberty, narcissism was intensified, especially in those favoured with good looks. They bring "a certain self-contentment", and the need to be loved takes precedence over the need to love. Certainly, as a rule, a man is aroused by what, for him, is the woman's attractiveness, and the woman by the fact that she can arouse the man. This does not mean that many women do not love in accordance with the masculine type, and more than a few men in line with the feminine. I have tried to clarify some of Freud's views on these matters elsewhere (Yorke, 1991), but his later comments, especially on the woman's mothering of the man (Freud, 1933a) and the break-up of the relationship with the first baby, are notable.

It seems worth adding that Freud considered that the narcissism of beautiful women, over and above their aesthetic attraction, holds a fascination for men who have renounced part of their own narcissism in a search for object love. He suggested that the self-assurance of cats, humorists, and criminals, as represented in literature, attracts by its narcissistic self-confidence; while small children also have a narcissistic charm in their self-contentment and inaccessibility. The woman's narcissistic beauty is envied as if for "maintaining a blissful state of mind—an unassailable libidinal position which we ourselves have since abandoned" (1914c, p. 89). But women may also love through attachment if a man has the kind of masculinity she has renounced. The categorization of types of object-choice set out in Freud's paper is, in my view, worth the closest scrutiny and says much about character.

A *sense of identity* is not the same thing as character; feminine disposition is not to be equated with female identity, or masculinity with male identity. A woman may refer to another as an "honorary man", or say of a boy "he should have been a girl". And men have equivalent, if less polite, terms for comparable kinds of men and women. It's as if people somehow *know* that a man may lack masculinity or a woman femininity, without being able to say too much about either of these qualities. But if we wish to explore their relationship to sexual *identity*, we encounter a real difficulty. Most militant feminists accept anatomical differences as fact but regard masculinity and femininity as social and cultural constructs, put together in the interests of control or constraint by men; they do not, as a rule, accept the concept of intrinsic bisexuality. Women analysts might be expected to know better. But, in analysis, unconscious penis envy in women and, in men, a passive[12] or feminine attitude to another man, only enter awareness with difficulty. An analyst who does not believe in either, or whose own analysis has failed in this respect, is only too likely to overlook evidence of their presence. Child analysts have long ago confirmed that, normally, a boy clings to his masculinity from the beginning, and that the wish to be masculine is, for girls, normal enough in the phallic phase, before it is subject to repression (but see the qualification below). The wish for a baby, and a husband or partner, may successfully replace the wish for a penis, though the wish for moth-

[12] The passive attitude is vigorously opposed because "it presupposes an acceptance of castration"—Freud (1937c), p. 251.

erhood may stem from a pre-oedipal identification with a baby, without any wish for a man to help to raise it.

Freud recognized the importance of envy in the male, exemplified in the wish of "Little Hans" to be able to have babies like his mother and to possess a penis that would in no way be inferior to his father's (Freud, 1909b). Nevertheless, Freud recognized that his theories of female development were centred too closely on his investigations of the male, and in trying to put this right, the findings of women colleagues were very helpful. Since then, there have been important modifications and elaborations on the concept. This is particularly true of penis envy. Edgcumbe and Burgner (1975) distinguished between the girl's phallic–narcissistic and phallic–oedipal phases, following previous work on early object relations (Burgner & Edgcumbe, 1972a, 1972b) and followed by a paper on the female negative oedipal phase (Edgcumbe, 1976). The 1975 contribution (which impressed Anna Freud) suggested that penis envy was a normal part of the phallic–narcissistic phase, but that entry into the phallic–oedipal phase normally meant that penis envy had been successfully dealt with (*already*, and successfully, repressed): the wish to possess has been replaced by the wish to receive. Persistence of the former during this later phase was strongly linked with such external factors as the absence of a father or the failure of the mother to offer a suitable model for feminine identification.

However this may be, some female psychoanalysts, and not a few male ones, have tried to deal with the enigma of masculinity and femininity by refusing to speak of *sexual identity* at all. Phyllis Tyson (1998), in an editorial introduction to a number of papers on the psychology of women, refers to Freud's remark that the psychological issues a woman faces are not limited to sexuality. That is undeniable, but the specification "woman" surely points to a sexual identity. Tyson goes on to say that the tendency to equate sexuality and identity is a "holdover" from the days when issues related to one's biological sex were put "under the rubric of *sexual identity*" (p. 361; Tyson's emphasis). She believes that the term *gender identity*—widely adopted by so many analysts—is more representative of the biological, physiological, sociological, genetic, and other factors that go to make up one's sense of identity. She sees, however, that the word "gender" has become "the politically correct term for biological sex", and that "this semantic shift has occasioned a loss of the psychological implications the term once carried with regard to the sense of identity". She fails, however, to note that the introduction of the term "gender" was itself a violation of the English language. "Gender" had always referred, not to people, but to substantives, to nouns, which can be designated as masculine, feminine, or neuter, depending on the language concerned. The *Oxford English Dictionary*, after noting this meaning with all due references and quotations, contains this entry:

> 3. *Transf.* Sex. [a] Now only *jocular*. b. In mod. (esp. feminist) use, a euphemism for the sex of a human being, often intended to emphasize the social and cultural, as opposed to the biological, distinctions between the sexes. [2nd ed. Vol. VI, p. 428]

As so often happens when language is manipulated for political purposes, a valuable distinction has been lost.[13]

Lastly, analysts who feel ill at ease in accepting the *fact* of sexual identity (why else want to replace it?) might draw comfort from Shengold (1989), who addresses Freud's question (noted in Jones's biography): "what does a woman want?" His answer is that *people*—men and women alike—want *everything*, and attempts to show that this is rooted in a primordial unity of sexuality in a striving for erotic merger with the mothering experience. It is of course pure fantasy: unconscious, archaic, mythical. It gains if read together with the opening chapters of Shengold's 1991 book (1991b). Whatever else, this work repays close scrutiny; but, for all the unifying sound of its conclusions, it contains no thought of doing away with "sexual identity".

Openness and rigidity

Certain character traits that, to my knowledge, have not hitherto been discussed psychoanalytically are readily detected in everyday life and concern the degree of openness and of ease in talking

---

[13] The fact that most of us sometimes fall into this error does not invalidate the point.

about oneself—in circumstances, that is, where this is appropriate.[14] The qualification is important, since even the most "open" of persons shows discretion. It seems to me that the open character is seen at its best when able to gauge, sometimes very quickly, the sensitivity of the listener. A casual and brief encounter may not be the right occasion to put forward observations, recollections, and opinions in a way that one would to a close friend. But, even when formalities alone are quite enough, an open character may reveal itself through an air of frankness, lack of artifice, spontaneity of expression, or even an appropriately amusing remark. These abilities will never amount to the recklessly gregarious: that would amount to a lack of sensitivity alien to the type of personality I have in mind.

But I refer, of course, to a spectrum: at the opposite end is concealment—people who never give anything away and confine any remarks to the bare minimum demanded by the occasion. They are reserved even with friends, who are rarely close and are selected on the grounds of common interests rather than personality. Any conversation tends to be restricted to the matters that bring them together; and if a friend is inclined to be more open, revelations may not be invited. The closed character will avoid any truly personal references to himself and, consciously or not, excludes from his own awareness any distasteful thoughts or anything that might fail to meet his ideas of what is proper to himself. If people at either end of the spectrum are not often found in pure culture, every degree between them is encountered, and the admixture of traits that goes to make up the characters of those concerned shows every kind of variation.

The rigid character may superficially resemble massive social inhibition. The latter, however, is often compatible with a wish to change, a longing to be able to speak more freely, to mix more readily, and even to be able to *enjoy* social exchange. A rigid character, however, is different in these respects and may not seem, to its proprietor, to be in any way out of order.

We can, perhaps, understand open and closed characters if we keep in mind the concept of the "repression barrier". Freud did

[14] This section draws on ideas first put forward in the British Institute of Psycho-Analysis *News* (Yorke, 1998).

not, as far as I know, use this expression, though he implied its existence, and it is now a matter of rather wider currency. The barrier is slow in its development; defence mechanisms such as denial appear earlier, say, than reaction formations, and these in turn precede yet others; the formation of secondary process occurs gradually; and the (hypothetical) hallucinatory wish-fulfilment has a long way to go before more complex thinking can more readily assist social advancement. Much needs to happen before the first five years or so of tempestuous life become subject to "infantile amnesia" and impervious to the most searching introspection, though family stories, photographs, and imperfect recollections of a few isolated events may give a semblance of early memory. But every child analyst knows that access to repressed material, before the barrier is formed, is so much easier than it is during latency.

The passing of the Oedipus complex and, with it, the emergence of a stable and structured childhood superego[15] is mainly responsible for the consolidation of a divide between two psychological phases. But it is *memory* that is cut off: the first few years of life continue, as we know, to exercise a compelling effect on all future development. All subsequent thinking, feeling, and action are influenced by those first formative years, the derivatives and outcome of which have passed into the system Unconscious.

All this is well known: what, however, is its bearing on character? I think it is this. If the divide is too firmly structured and almost totally impermeable, *a rigid character structure develops*, and both social and personal adaptation is severely impaired. If the repression barrier is less impregnable and open to breaches acceptable to the superego and compatible with ego functioning, then the more comfortable adaptations permitted by open-mindedness are available to the personality and form an important—very important—part of *character*. Infantile amnesia itself is intact, but freedom of social intercourse, the accessibility of all kinds of material in jokes (subject to the reality testing of *taste*), and the ability to play with young children *in mutual enjoyment*, not to speak of the capacity for healthy (if not always fearless) introspection, point to an open character. And to this may be added, *inter alia*, in those

[15] The superego still has to undergo major changes in adolescence.

suitably gifted, the emergence of otherwise unconscious material in the guise of art: all these qualities may become invaluable personal attributes.

Concluding remarks

Character is beyond the confines of any colloquium. It embraces far too much: the entire history of the individual and his internal and external relationships is contained within it. It is no sense a hopeless subject for psychoanalytic study: the subject is altogether massive, and much remains unknown, as it does about mental functioning in general. I have tried, then, to do no more than make a few observations on what, broadly, is already known.

The quotation from Henry James at the head of this chapter points to the complexities of character. "Observation" has many facets and in most circumstances is counted a virtue. A lack of it is rarely an advantage. But, in this instance, Tony Bream is told (whether or not ironically) that it suits his character perfectly—in effect, that conjoined with his other character traits, the result is right for him. The alleged lack of observation does not, in his case, amount to an inhibition of curiosity, as it might in some. As in so much of James, the quotation contains paradox and contradiction, themselves no strangers to character.

CHAPTER FIVE

Of teeth and theft and Poe: non-Lacanian purloining

Ronnie Bailie

In Charles Baudelaire, Edgar Allan Poe—newly dead and released at last from the insoluble problem of gratitude—founda dazzlingly eloquent and passionate advocate. In one memorable outburst, the great French poet denounced the "vampire–pedagogue" and called for a by-law "to keep dogs out of cemeteries" (Baudelaire, 1856). He had in mind in particular the violence done to Poe's memory immediately after his death by Rufus Griswold and did not pause to reflect that Poe had—for reasons to which we will come—assiduously created enemies for the greater part of his short life. Viewed from the closing years of the twentieth century, the outburst has, notwithstanding, its posthumous justness. For while full-length biographies of Poe continue to appear (Myers, 1992; Silverman, 1991) and while he continues to be read and to provoke the extreme reactions in which he took no little pleasure, psychoanalysis, despite the auspicious beginning represented by the work of Marie Bonaparte (Bonaparte, 1933), has in the main—paradoxically—failed to do justice to a man whose life seems almost to have been created for psychoanalytic investigation. This has been, in essence—to continue Baudelaire's metaphor—because his body has been stolen, which is to say, less fancifully, that it has dropped out of the question because the peculiar emphases of Lacanian psychoanalysis have, for some decades now, dominated psychological approaches to Poe.

It is, therefore, with some aptness that Muller and Richardson's 1988 volume of essays is called *The Purloined Poe,* for while it admits dissenting and variant voices—such as those of Marie Bonaparte and Norman Holland—the collection is unashamedly Lacanian in inspiration and in its approach to "The Purloined Letter", this being, of course, the tale of Poe that most excited Lacan's interest and motivated the famous seminar of 1956 (Lacan, 1966). Now the striking problem about this, from the perspective of the present writer, is that, in essence, Lacan makes Poe's tale of theft into a parable about meaning. He then rises on the wings of a pun ["*vol*": theft/flight] that Poe's native language declines to endorse, seizes on the idea of flight, and links it with the mobility of the (endlessly displaced and variable) signifier that the stolen letter becomes for the characters in the tale. Now whatever the intellectual virtuosity of Lacan's performance and whatever the fascinations of the debate he has provoked, the fact remains that ordinary theft and associated conscious and unconscious ideas about theft were of enormous psychological significance to Poe. As long ago as 1926, Joseph Wood Krutch reminded us that plagiarism was one of Poe's "manias". In the following remarks I wish, therefore, summarily to set aside the "disincarnated subject" (Roustang, 1986) created by Lacanian readers of Poe and reconsider a Poe to whom both a personal history and an individual body have been restored. This will lead us to a view of "The Purloined Letter" in which the idea of theft is accorded a concrete reality.

It is well known that Poe lost his mother, an itinerant actress, to tuberculosis in December 1811. There is every reason to suppose that the child of 35 months had closely witnessed her decline, for the stories of his adulthood are littered with unaccountable details that do not seem referable to conscious memory. His hapless father had deserted the ill-starred family some time before, and with the loss of a second parent Edgar and his two siblings found themselves dispersed, Edgar passing into the childless home of John Allan, a prosperous merchant in Richmond. While Edgar was able to develop a good relationship with Allan's sickly wife, Frances, his relationship with Allan was a troubled one, and, as I hope to show, almost certainly the source of his lifelong inability to get along with men. As Krutch remarks, Poe was to become a man "with whom it was almost impossible to deal". Allan, of modest Scottish origin, was—and prided himself in being—a self-made man: in spite of having in William Galt a prodigiously wealthy uncle who was later to leave him a fortune, he was most conscious of having risen by his own efforts. Regretting his own lack of education, and with some pretensions to gentility, he evidently proposed to give his ward the liberal education that had eluded *him*. That there was some narcissistic investment in this enterprise is neither obscure nor surprising; but that the relationship was—from the outset, and even before it was a question of Edgar as a particular person—not free from a marked ambivalence is clear in the fact that the child, unlike his brother and sister, was not (and was never to be) legally adopted. We know that Allan was capable of being liberal, generous, and indulgent with the pretty child who entered his household in 1812; at the other extreme, we also know that by the time the 17-year-old Edgar was at the University of Virginia, adequate financial support was denied him, and soon afterwards the relationship had broken down irretrievably. And we also know that the years in-between were the scene of numerous conflicts. It is most important for an understanding of Poe to know why.

The central fact seems to be that John Allan was a man for whom the act of giving was deeply problematic: in him the impulse to give and the impulse to withhold were precariously balanced. Part of him—no doubt the part to which Edgar was a narcissistic object—seemed to say, "I will give you what I was never given"; but another part, the part raised in a Spartan regime by his wealthy uncle, who was visibly more generous with orphans than with his own relation, evidently resented the child and asked "Why should I give to you what I was not given?" Since the evidence clearly suggests that things got steadily worse as Edgar got older, we may suspect that Edgar progressively ceased to be pleasing to Allan as he began to develop individuality and autonomy, for the cardinal "sin" of the narcissistic object is to disclose itself as separate, as undeniably other (Fliess, 1961).

Edgar's troubled relationship with Allan was to mark irreversibly his relationships with men. And it was not simply to be a question of conflict with men who withheld things from him. For he quarrelled both with those from whom he needed something (a job, a favour, money) and, more perniciously, with any man who had *given him something* or been kind to him. Of all these, Allan was the fatal prototype.

We can cast an additional light on these matters by turning to Poe's correspondence. Here is a passage from a letter that Edgar wrote to Allan in his early days (there were never to be any late ones) at the University of Virginia: he is describing a fight between two of his fellow students, one of whom

> after getting the other completely in his power began to bite— I saw the arm afterward—and it really was a serious matter.—It was bitten from the shoulder to the elbow—and it is likely that pieces of flesh as large as my hand will be obliged to be cut out. [Ostrom, 1966]

This is as good an example of writing for effect, or manipulating the reader's feelings, as one could find in the tales for which he later became famous. The attempt to have Allan worry, indeed to alarm him, is almost indistinguishable from reproach at having sent him to such a place. But of greater interest still is the curious fact that Poe's account of the incident seems haunted by the English locution, "to bite the hand that feeds you". Here we can take the measure of his gratitude to Allan. As we shall see, Poe's hostility often displayed an oral–sadistic character, and something of the ferocity of his conscious and unconscious feeling about his guardian is betrayed both in his choice of this incident to relay to him and in the graphic terms in which he found himself describing it.

A few years later, following his disastrous experiments with army life and finally alienated from the Allan household, Poe's wanderings took him to Baltimore and into the home of his dead father's widowed sister, Maria Clemm. Baudelaire remarked that Poe might appropriately have had the words "No Luck" emblazoned on his forehead. Mrs Clemm was the unquestionable exception that the Gods allowed. In her, Poe found a reciprocated maternal attachment that was to last beyond his short life. She was a woman without means or intelligence, but who found a prodigious energy of devotion for the penniless wanderer who one day appeared at her door. When, four years later, he married her 13-year-old daughter, Virginia, the three constituted the only real home that Edgar was ever to know. It is important to add that he was the only man in that home, which brings us to another cardinal fact about Poe. With the few women he was close to, his relations were completely free of the overt and often rather dramatic conflicts that poisoned his associations with men. Whatever the changes of place and circumstance, many visitors came away with the same impression, that Edgar was the adored centre of the household—to both Maria and his wife Virginia, whose attentions to him reminded at least one visitor of a "young mother" with her "first-born" (Quinn, 1941). Strikingly, as in the tales, the erotic motive is consistently missing from all accounts of this domestic scene. With women, Poe sought relationships that were comforting and sustaining, relationships, if one will, of an oral dependent type. As Krutch convincingly argues, Poe's choice of Virginia was at bottom the choice of an impossible partner, a partner, that is, with whom any physical consummation of the relationship could decently be set aside. It is difficult to escape the allied suspicion that a powerful inhibition on sexual activity was indeed an important part of Poe's make-up. But this leads us to the further reflection that his real relations with women were cordial and harmonious *because they were being shielded* from ideas and fantasies that (he feared) sexual activity would have brought into play. One has only to think of the extraordinary and often gruesome fates of the heroines of many of the stories to be struck by the contrast between them and the domestic sweetness in which it appears they were conceived.

* * *

When you enter Poe's stories, you enter his imagination: you also come closer to his psychic realities. Curiously, there comes a point at which, compared to the imagined world, the facts of his life, however compelling, only serve to delay insight. And even by the eccentric standards of Poe's work, "Berenice" is an exceedingly strange tale, from the very beginning considered of questionable taste. For at its climax is an act of theft, in the form of dental surgery performed on a corpse—the corpse of a beloved long-ailing cousin. It is worth noting and holding fast to the fact that "Berenice" was the first imaginative fruit of Poe's marriage to his cousin Virginia in 1836 and provides unrivalled evidence as to the fantasies that evidently attended that event. (I say "fantasies" because the tuberculosis that Virginia contracted did not declare itself until six years later: her unconscious psychic representation to her husband was, of course, another matter.) "Berenice" is assuredly not a tale of connubial bliss.

Aegeus, the brooding narrator of the piece, dreams his life away in the family library: we see him nowhere else. His dominant memories are of his cousin Berenice's early zest and vitality and her precipitate decline. This sounds reasonably straightforward, but the library-world, however atmospherically appropriate, inverts the nature of his reality: in truth he does not inhabit the world of adult thought and language but a peculiar world of magical thinking, mired in the single implacable question, "What have I done?" He has an unconscious conviction that Berenice's decline is really a matter of her having come to his attention. In this decline—in which he remotely suspects his own agency—his attention fixes on her with greater and greater intensity and settles with something like fascination upon her teeth. Poe is most insistent on the circumstance that it is not that he *thinks* about her teeth, or about her. It is, rather, a question of an arrest of thinking, an inhibition of thought. As the story (obscurely) states: "[Her teeth] became the essence of my mental life." One might say that his rapt awareness of them stands in the place of a free mental life. But we can decipher further this condensed and primitive logic: the teeth are instead of thoughts and represent the thoughts that Aegeus cannot have; in addition, the thoughts that he cannot have are thoughts about teeth. The reader of the story will find the narrator's mental state encoded also in the curious lacunae that punctuate the text, rendered typographically by suspension points. These absences—as if bits have simply fallen out of the story—mark what cannot be remembered or thought. In so far as Aegeus may be said to think, his thought is merely the notation of the absence of thought. Representationally speaking, the story is thus a paradox: wordy, intricate, analytic, abstruse, it assembles the pseudo-thoughts of a man who cannot think.

The question why Berenice's teeth—and not some other part of her body—are selected for special attention is an important one. If we remind ourselves that Elizabeth Poe died when Edgar was 35 months old, at least two things come to mind. The final stages of tuberculosis involve a number of striking outward physical changes in the sufferer, including extreme emaciation. Sometimes facial emaciation is so pronounced that the skin may be pierced by the cheekbones; wastage of the lips and recession of the gums may lend a skull-like prominence and visibility to the teeth. "Berenice" is by no means the only story that may well have been influenced by unconscious memories of things young Edgar (as I have noted) almost certainly observed around his mother's deathbed: the strange guttural whisper in "William Wilson" is another striking example, recalling the continual hoarseness and inability to speak above a whisper characteristic of a sufferer in whom the disease has ulcerated the throat (Rothman, 1995). Ill-defined, elusive memories of real events, observed but not understood, may be suspected behind many of Poe's stories, lending them a quality of poignant evocativeness that is the reverse of mystification. For in a very real sense, the things to be remembered, far from being hidden, were never known. And so with the accent on teeth in "Berenice". But in the view of the present writer, the dental imagery of the tale is overdetermined in at least one other way.

If we ask ourselves at what stage of Edgar's psychological and emotional development he found himself witnessing his once lively and singing mother's decline and death, we are, weighing the evidence, likely to place these events in the later oral phase. As Ruth and Thomas Freeman have pointed out (Freeman & Freeman, 1992), the anatomical record lends clear theoretical and chronological support to Abraham's (1924) refinement of Freud's libido theory (1905d) in which the oral phase is subdivided into an earlier stage, associated with sucking and whose (benign) sexual aim is incorporation, and a later oral sadistic stage associated with biting and characterized by a sexual aim of destroying the object. Since the full set of (deciduous) teeth has not erupted before 30 months, nor is the concomitant musculoskeletal development before then complete, it seems reasonable to suggest that oral sadistic trends become most pronounced in the middle of the third year of life. The main psychological importance of the oral sadistic phase is, of course, that it marks a new attitude of ambivalence towards the object, an ambivalence subsequently extended into the anal sadistic phase. The core pathogenic problem of such ambivalence is nicely formulated by Fairbairn (1952): "how to love without destroying by hate". One defence against the associated fantasies of destruction (or biting) is regression to the earlier, preambivalent oral stage with its benign aim of (preservative) incorporation by sucking. The vacillation in Poe's fiction—which is only to say, in his socialized fantasy—between the wish to destroy and the wish to preserve (embodied most characteristically in the recurring fantasy of the woman buried but alive) is so striking that it is reasonable to allow it some evidentiary value in the above argument. And it is the same oral ambivalence that is echoed in his life by a well-attested verbal charm and an even better-documented—and at times quite extraordinary—verbal severity.

All of which, aside from its intimate connection with the psychogenesis of "Berenice", leads us to the assertion that Edgar Poe was almost certainly at the height of his infantile oral sadism when his mother declined and died, and to the further likelihood that this real object loss was unconsciously registered by the child as an act of murder. For to the primitive ego, loss is not simple misfortune: it is a hated act of desertion and/or overwhelming evidence of the destructive potential of the self. Such fearful causal association ("I had done a deed—What was it?") stealthily rules the thought-free world of Aegeus. As we have seen, *ideas* about teeth—still less the idea of biting to death—are not admitted into the text: they are the unthinkable; they are precisely that on account of which there may be no thought. Only the remorseless image of teeth—isolated from its unconscious context—is admitted as the symbolic representative of such unthought ideas.

One of the most remarkable things about "Berenice" is the consistency with which it is misread. By this I do not mean "misinterpreted", for what but divergent views of a story so bizarre might one expect? By "misread" I mean that commentators invariably misdescribe the sequence of events in the climactic graveyard sequence. Accounts typically imply that Aegeus, with his grizzly dental surgery, murders his beloved whom he discovers alive in her coffin. These are the improvisations of readers. On the (reasoned) assumption that the "thinking" in and behind the story is primitive and concrete, we must in all simplicity believe that Berenice is indeed dead when she is laid to rest. When Aegeus violates the grave in order to steal her teeth, it is not that he discovers her alive: it is, rather, that *she becomes alive* by dint of having her teeth removed. For the act of apparent desecration is in essence an *undoing* performed in the magical thought world of the reversible. To summarize: in the opening sequence of the story, the unavailable and intolerable unconscious thought that the love object has been destroyed by biting is overlaid by an obsessed but *unthinking* vision of her teeth; at the end of the tale, this in its turn is exchanged for the facile magical thought that the removal of (her) teeth will set all to rights. *It does not*, for the overwhelming affects released in this imaginative experiment—this trial thought—prove far beyond mastery. (As we shall shortly see, at bottom this is because the "magical" solution *is itself an act of theft*.) You can call these terrible feelings, duly orchestrated as fiction, "Gothic horror" and dissolve them in a familiar cultural product; or you can reflect that, for Edgar Poe, so often thought of as a forger of emotions, the Gothic literary repertoire provided *on the contrary* convenient masquerades in which he could present his core realities *as if they* were a series of fabrications. However bizarre, "Berenice" is a faithful, almost *literal* unconscious commentary on the massive anxieties that lay beneath the domestic sweetness that characterized Poe's life, and especially his married life, with the Clemms, mother and daughter.

* * *

Let us remind ourselves that we are on a path that must lead us back to "The Purloined Letter" and questions of theft, and note in passing that in "Berenice" the lurid act of theft with which it culminates is passed over in relative silence and attracts no special notice or thought: only the associated emotions of horror and terrified disbelief are admitted. On the other hand, as I have already remarked, Poe did not preserve a tactful silence in *all* matters to do with theft; and here we return to the large question of plagiarism. This had exclusively to do with Poe's relations to men and followed a pattern so consistent and so irrational that the contribution from the side of psychopathology is inescapable. In general, Poe was not one to let reality stand in the way of his convictions, and this is so *a fortiori* in his plagiarism madness. Even the saintly forbearance of a Longfellow, baselessly accused by Poe of plagiarism, was insufficient to deflect him from the inflexible course of accusation once he was embarked upon it.

Poe's *misfortunes* are very well documented, but in countless editorial and other positions on the little magazines of his day, and in other circumstances also, he was the recipient of many kindnesses. He had the utmost difficulty in accepting these with a good grace. Friendships with men tended to begin cordially enough, and it was often, quite naturally, a question of employment, credit, helpfulness, or favour extended to the unquestionably needy and often perfectly indigent Poe. The benefactor was usually, in the nature of things, a figure of authority or (at least in fantasy) the custodian of plenty: at all events, someone from whom Poe *needed* something. Kindnesses once received, there followed seemingly inevitable feelings of disillusionment on Poe's part, often recriminations, and then an attack that included, whenever possible, the accusation of plagiarism or literary theft. One does not put the case too strongly in referring to this (with Krutch) as one of Poe's obsessions, a term that usefully sets one to wondering what thoughts were sealed up behind it. There is no doubt that when relations with men began to sour—as sour they invariably did—this particular accusation was the choicest weapon in his limited arsenal. The psychically sensitive or intolerable thing was evidently the condition of having been given something by a man and consequently finding himself in a situation in which gratitude might have been an appropriate response. (Dostoevsky could almost have claimed Poe for an acquaintance when he remarked in *Notes From Underground* that a human being was someone with "two legs and no sense of gratitude".) Unsurprisingly, Poe's difficulty with gratitude did not go unremarked by his contemporaries:

> One of the strange parts of his strange nature was to entertain a spirit of revenge toward all who did him a service. . . . He rarely, or never, failed to malign those who befriended him. [Myers, 1992]

What are we to make of all of this? There seems little doubt that, at bottom, we are dealing with the defence of projection. The vehement recurring accusation (and, indeed, unshakeable conviction) that *a man had stolen* or *had stolen from him* must have had its source in an unconscious belief that it was *he* who was guilty of grievous indefensible theft. This intolerable idea sought transient relief in projections so unavailing that they had always to be renewed. But as we pick our steps along the labyrinthine (co)determinants of this state of affairs, we remind ourselves that, as regards plagiarism, Poe, as is well attested in the literature, had stolen much, and often brazenly. I am sure that he did not acknowledge all of these thefts to himself, though it seems equally clear that with others—the brazen variety—he was "perfectly" aware of (what he told himself) he was doing. This latter manoeuvre he was able to perform without psychological inconsistency: for he told himself he was *not stealing*, just playing a trick on any reader too stupid to unmask it. None of these elucidations serve, however, to furnish us with an answer to the greater, more imposing question that looms implacably behind them. Why was the idea of having stolen so intolerable and threatening that it called forth such urgent elemental defences and the recurring projective behaviour consequent on them? Why, in other words, was so much psychic energy caught up in this issue?

Part of the answer to this question undoubtedly takes us back to John Allan, who had, we recall, first doted on the orphan he was later to reject and deny. While the general psychological situation in the household was such as I have already set out, in order to understand Poe's extraordinary sensitivity to the issue of theft it is perhaps necessary to add something else and reconstruct Allan's likely interactions with his ward more concretely and circumstantially. Reading backwards from the plagiarism obsession, one could advance the plausible reconstruction that Allan was, from earliest times, in the habit of drawing Edgar's attention to what he had been given and raising the question of the degree to which he truly deserved such bounty. Hardly a paragon of tact or sensitivity, Allan must often have given the child the feeling that he did not deserve what he had been given, that, being as he was, behaving as he did, he had come by it falsely: for, after all, his birthright was precisely nothing. The mere taking of what was (so ambivalently) given could thus have been stealthily invested with the character of *theft*. It is also possible, of course—the adult Poe being in reality a plagiarist—that Edgar engaged in real acts of (petty) theft, or symbolic theft, in the household and that the plainest of accusations were on occasion levelled against him. This makes me think of Winnicott's remark about the child's search for the one (usually mother) from whom he has the right to steal (Winnicott, 1957).

But, however something along these lines may have contributed to the "plagiarism complex" that characterized Poe's adult years, the need for defensive recapitulation—through projection—of real relations to objects can only have been a codeterminant of such a morbid sensitization of the area of giving and taking. On the level of the drives, it is important to connect this issue with the other evidence of oral sadistic fixations that we have already considered. In his 1924 paper, Abraham makes reference to the occurrence of kleptomania in a number of (female) oral sadistic patients, a point picked up by Ruth and Thomas Freeman (1992). It seems to the present writer that *taking from* the object, had, in unconscious fantasy, become for Poe the psychic equivalent of *destroying* the object, and "theft"—representing the essence of what was bad about him—was thus to be repudiated at all costs. That is why the—ostensibly superficial—issue of plagiarism reverberated to the core of his being. Behind it was a ferocious oral sadistic fantasy involving the destruction of a primary object. And it is, of course, precisely this fantasy (and its reparative adjuncts) that is compulsively repeated in and indeed drives the stories—but only on certain conditions, as rigidly observed as, and psychically the equivalent of, Poe's avoidance of sexual activity. Hatred of a woman is *never allowed direct expression;* only her destruction is as consistent as this absence of avowed hatred. In its absence, this hatred may only be symbolized: by disease ("The Fall of the House of Usher"), by hatred of a man [it is a man not a woman that I hate]("The Cask of Amontillado"), and/or by theft from a woman, as in "Berenice" and "The Purloined Letter". And we can now see that "Berenice" is constructed around a psychological impasse. Murderous teeth can only be removed by an act of theft that has become the psychic equivalent of that same destructiveness.

Some additional confirmation of these views may be found in the extreme mental states that the abuse of alcohol induced in Poe in the last pitiful months of his life. We are indebted to his friend, the engraver John Sartain, for various detailed accounts of the delusions and hallucinations that Poe experienced while briefly confined to prison for drunkenness in Philadelphia in late June and early July of 1849. In one hallucinatory episode, he was compelled to witness the mutilation of his "mother, Mrs Clemm" [*sic*] in the form of a systematic sawing off of her limbs, joint by joint, starting from the feet. That the instrument of destruction of the female should be a (toothed) saw is strikingly appropriate. Moreover, in an earlier part of the same hallucinated sequence, a sequence curiously riddled with reminiscences of *Hamlet*, "a young female brightly radiant" appeared to him "on the battlements" of the prison and whispered questions that it was a matter of life and death he should hear and answer. He next narrowly avoids being immersed by a prison guard "up to the lips" in boiling liquid. This signalling of the mouth leads into the next scene, in which his persecutors "blast [his] sight" with the sawing up of Mrs Clemm. The wronged and suffering figure in these eloquent fragments is consistently a woman, first the ghost-like young woman appearing on the battlements (in the place of the murdered king/father of *Hamlet*) to address her terrified son, or the young mother's later representative, Maria Clemm.

Released from the Philadelphia prison without a fine, Poe next tried to make his way back to New York and the protection of Maria. But while she was always an actual and internally represented source of comfort and security to Edgar, she was also, as the hallucinations released by organic distress clearly indicate, a figure of anxiety, herself in need of protection from her "wolfish" son (Ostrom, 1966). Not surprisingly, unconscious processes made his wish to return to her at this time an area of conflict:

> He said that it would be difficult for me to believe what he had to tell, or that such things were possible in this nineteenth century. . . . He told me he had been on his way to New York, but he had heard some men who sat a few seats back of him plotting how they should kill him and then throw him off the platform of the car. He said they spoke so low that it would have been impossible for him to hear and understand the meaning of their words, had it not been that his sense of hearing was so wonderfully acute. [Krutch, 1926]

The delusions of reference and persecution were powerful enough to cause Poe to abandon his return to Maria, get off the train, and return to Philadelphia, where he presented himself in a state of extreme agitation at John Sartain's studio and asked for a razor to remove his moustache in order to elude his assassins. Once again, we note that the mouth is selected for special emphasis in these delusional phenomena, appearing both as the focus of what is destructive in the assassins (whispered speech) and as the means for eluding destruction if something dangerous is removed (the moustache). It is not surprising that, when Sartain enquired what the men in the train had against Poe, he replied that it was a matter of revenge over "a woman trouble" (Silverman, 1991). Appropriately, in the days that followed, Sartain noted that, before they remitted, the delusions of persecution alternated with the idea of *self*-destruction—a circumstance strongly suggestive of the reinternalization of superego elements embodied in his imagined persecutors while the psychotic episode lasted.

* * *

We now arrive at "The Purloined Letter" by way of a detour that has alerted us to the importance of theft in Poe's psychopathology. While the idea of theft finds its way into a number of Poe's stories, "The Purloined Letter" is unique for promoting it to an almost flamboyant centrality. In saying this, I am not merely thinking of the title but of the particularly brazen, almost *advertised* theft that the story takes as its heart. It is also necessary to speak in the plural: for while Minister D's theft from the Queen, right under her nose, is the prime mover of the plot, Dupin's retrieval of the letter is, as we shall see, a theft in its own right, and just as advertised. This begins to suggest the complication of the story, which is a labyrinth, and indeed, to speak plainly, a deliberate snare for the reader. For even as, Dupin leading, it parades its logical rigour, its imperturbable reasonableness, its simplicity—all the while a subversion of these things is underway, right under *our* noses. We are not merely witnesses (readers) of this truly remarkable and deeply perfidious story about cunning and devious people but implicated in it by the act of reading, because we also—we especially—are duped as we read, cheated out of our trust and intellectually fleeced. Krutch's memorable phrase is worth repeating: Poe was a man "with whom it was almost impossible to deal". "The Purloined Letter" achieves the remarkable feat of putting us in a real relation with Poe. It reads like an act of revenge, and we come away from it burnt and indignant.

But none of this—that Poe should rise from his tomb to demoralize us—stands in the way of the story's pretended benignity. Auguste Dupin is proposed from the outset as a man of great perspicacity, and a perspicacity occasionally pressed into public service when the Parisian constabulary are, as now, baffled by a crime. As citizens, we thus forgive him his ironic hauteur and make nothing of his love of darkness, nor the curious fact that, as the story opens, he—later so garrulous—first materializes to us out of a long *silence*. When he is informed by his perplexed visitor that the Queen is endangered by the theft of a private letter, he appears to offer what advice he can to the troubled Prefect of Police. After all, before the story is over, he will state his political allegiances openly: "I act as a partisan of the lady concerned." Moreover, it is not to be denied that it is by his agency and his acumen alone that the letter is making its way back to the Queen as the story ends. On one level Dupin may thus be said to rescue the "exalted personage" from her predicament. And in this respect he stands in exact counterpoint to the thieving Minister D, whom we have no difficulty in seeing as the clever but quite unscrupulous and ruthless villain of the piece. As Dupin intimates, the thieving minister is a man who is perfectly capable murder. If we view Poe's likely psychological investment in the tale in the light of our thinking thus far, the formula seems relatively simple. Minister D represents the force of theft and destruction and Dupin both the externalizing defence ("It was *he* who stole, not I.") and the reparative impulse ("On the contrary, I *undid* the harm he caused."). In other words, we have in essence returned to the psychological terrain of plagiarism by way of a fictional representation of that area of Poe's unconscious processes.

"The Purloined Letter" does not, however, consent to be limited by the contours of unimpeached wish-fulfilment. The trouble is, of course, that the detective Dupin—as befits the most *knowing* denizen of the Rue Dûnot—is a much more complicated and paradoxical individual than he is acknowledged to be. Many details stealthily gnaw at the reader's peace, and most of these have to do with the resemblance between the Minister and Dupin (Muller & Richardson, 1988). There is first the alphabetic perversity of naming in which not merely the letter (epistle) but the letter "D" unites them. It is casually pointed out that both are poets. Their respective acts of theft closely mirror one another: D gives specious cover to the original theft from the Queen by openly substituting a letter that to a degree resembles the one purloined. The audacious substitution of a imperfect simulacrum is precisely the tactic adopted by Dupin for his stealing (back) of the letter. There is also the unsettling appearance of intimacy between the adversaries. This has to do with the (unexplained) extent of Dupin's knowledge of D, his habits, the circumstances of his life, his modes of thought, and also with his easy frequentation of the Minister's apartments, apparently without appointment. At one point it is even suggested that the Minister has a brother—a suggestion that Dupin summarily rebutts. Here the reader may recall that the term of the Queen's suffering is 18 months (or two gestations) and wonder whether a sly insinuation of literal fraternity rather than "mere" likeness is part of the tale's pattern of telling and concealment.

To find that Dupin resembles his unscrupulous adversary is, of course, to be thrown back on further scrunitizing all that has to do with Dupin himself. This, however, is something that one force acting in the story tries to preempt. After all, did ever man more thoroughly *explain himself* than Dupin when he talks? And yet there is that long opening smoke-filled silence and the fact that we (and his closest companion) are only *afterwards* privy to his crucial actions at the heart of the tale. Our talker moves as stealthily as the tale that encloses him. For example, nothing is less highlighted in "The Purloined Letter" than the chronology of events, but, on the other hand, everything is there to be pieced together. If we ask when Dupin solves the crime, we are compelled to conclude that he does so in the first moments of the Prefect's first visit. When, on the Prefect's second visit, Dupin hands him the stolen letter, a whole month has elapsed, and we have no reason to conclude that an even longer period of delay would have caused Dupin to *act* rather than to *wait* with the letter in his possession. The issue here is, of course, the apparently needless protraction of the Queen's suffering, the Queen as whose "partisan" Dupin claims to act. This brings us to the question of Dupin's motivation, the question of what he wants. While the simplifying distortions of memory might cause the reader to remember Dupin as a somewhat eccentric but essentially high-minded devotee of knowledge and sharp reasoning, the details of the story make the case for his disinterestedness quite unsustainable. While it is shrouded by a fair amount of intellectual smoke, there is simply no escaping the fact of our hero's venality. Concealing the fact that he has come into possession of the letter, his first demand is that a price be paid: he does not give but *sells* the letter to the Prefect. This is perhaps the core of his resemblance to the Minister and is, if one will, Dupin's secret: his protection of the "exalted personage" is a sham: he merely "acts" (the equivocating term is his own) as a partisan of the Queen and is actuated by desires that make him just as ruthless and destructive as his rival.

That is why the closing words of "The Purloined Letter"—emulating Dupin's habit of concealing and displaying at the same moment—present us with a teasing mirror image of two men:

> *Un dessein si funeste,*
> *S'il n'est digne d'Atrée, est digne de Thyeste.*

Thyestes and Atreus were, of course, brothers pitched in a bloody rivalry. Appropriately, in the myth, both a woman (Aërope, the wife of Atreus) and a stolen object (a golden ram, pledge of Atreus' rule) also figure. The perfidy of Thyestes is theft and seduction; that of Atreus, to serve up the children of Thyestes to him at a banquet. The fragment of French verse seems to indicate that, in a contest of morality, while there is little to choose between the brothers, Thyestes might have the edge in perfidiousness. What is intriguing about Poe's use of the quotation, however, is its insoluble ambiguity, for it is impossible to say whether the "fatal plan" is the Minister's original theft or Dupin's studious emulation of it. In other words, it is impossible to determine which of the men is Atreus (the seeker of a grisly revenge) and which is the instigating Thyestes. Moreover, the idea that either action might be "worthy" is lavishly ironic, whether in the myth or in Poe's tale. From the perspective of the present writer, there seems to be no end to the calculation that Poe put into the use of this epigraph, as into all aspects of this extraordinary story. And yet Poe could not have been conscious of the larger appropriateness that over-determined his (I imagine) deep satisfaction with the epigraph. For it referred the question of theft to its primitive psychic origins and restored it to the fantasied status of being "funeste" or fatal. The grotesque mythological image in which the loved are eaten must also have stirred his core fantasy of oral destructiveness.

There is a rather obvious intellectuality in "The Purloined Letter", far from such grisly feasts, and Dupin certainly wishes to appear to us in a cerebral light: he bids fair to be the man without a body, the "disincarnated subject" that we considered in opening and found impossible. For there is no escaping the fact that this is a defensive posture, nor the related fact that his desires cast their shadow over the tale, as all bodies cast shadows. At the heart of "The Purloined Letter" is a massive enterprise of repudiation, an enterprise in which Dupin is Poe's representative. It is theft of which they attempt the repudiation, theft understood not trivially but in the network of unconscious thinking that this essay attempts to sketch. To the force of projection, the villain is the other, is Minister D: but he becomes a mirror turning towards the smoke-obscured face of his "brother" Dupin. In addition to the force of self-justification, of self-exculpation, there is also something in the story that would gladly make "purloining" the letter's fate rather than a moment of that fate: there is, in other words, a force in the story that would gladly make thieving into a universal principle and thereby abolish the crime. But the need for these ingenious defences and evasions stands in the end as testimony to the psychically momentous, psychically critical character of "purloining" in the strange inner world of Edgar Poe. There an implacable unconscious logic stands aloof from Dupin's game and robs theft itself of all possible impunity.

REFERENCES

Abend, S. M. (1983). Theory of character. Panel Report. *Journal of the American Psychoanalytic Association, 31*: 211–224.

Abraham, K. (1924). A short view of the development of the libido, viewed in the light of mental disorders. In: *Selected Papers of Karl Abraham M.D.* London: Karnac Books, 1979.

Abrams, S. (1986). Disposition and environment. *Psychoanalytic Study of the Child, 41*: 41–60.

Abrams, S. (1991). Panellist's Comments. Twelfth International Scientific Colloquium, Anna Freud Centre. *Bulletin of the Anna Freud Centre, 14*: 213–218.

Aguayo, J. (1997). Historicising the origins of Kleinian psychoanalysis: Klein's analytic and patronal relationships with Ferenczi, Abraham and Jones, 1914–1927. *International Journal of Psycho-Analysis, 78*: 1165–1182.

Arlow, J. (1969). Unconscious fantasy and disturbances of conscious experience. *Psychoanalytic Quarterly, 38*: 1–27.

Amacher, P. (1965). Freud's neurological education and its influence on psychoanalytic theory. *Psychological Issues, 4* (Monograph 16).

Amacher, P. (1974). The concepts of the pleasure principle and infantile erogenous zones shaped by Freud's neurological education. *Psychoanalytic Quarterly, 43*: 218–223.

Baudelaire, C. (1856). Edgar Poe, sa vie et ses oeuvres. In: *Oeuvres Complètes*. 2 vols. Paris: Gallimard, 1976.

Baudry, F. (1983). The evolution of the concept of character in Freud's writings. *Journal of the American Psychoanalytic Association, 31*: 3–31.

Baudry, F. (1984). Character: a concept in search of an identity. *Journal of the American Psychoanalytic Association, 32*: 455–477.

Baudry, F. (1989). Character, character type, and character organization. *Journal of the American Psychoanalytic Association, 37*: 655–686.

Bion, W. (1957). Differentiation of the psychotic from the non-psychotic personalities. *International Journal of Psycho-Analysis, 38*: 266–275.

Bion, W. (1962). *Learning from Experience*. London: Karnac Books.

Bion, W. (1970). *Attention and Interpretation*. London: Karnac Books.

Bird, B. (1972). Notes on transference. *Journal of the American Psychoanalytic Association, 20*: 267–301.

Bleuler, E. (1911). *Dementia Praecox or the Group of Schizophrenias*. New York: International Universities Press, 1955.

Bonaparte, M. (1933). *Edgar Poe, sa vie—son oeuvre: étude analytique* (2 vols.). Paris: Editions Denoel et Steele.

Bohr, N. (1932). Light and life. In: *Atomic Physics and Human Knowledge. Vol. 2* (pp. 3–12). Woodbridge, CT: Ox Bow Press, 1958.

Brenner, C. (1974). On the nature and development of affects: a unified theory. *Psychoanalytic Quarterly, 43*: 532–556.

Brenner, C. (1976). *Psychoanalytic Technique and Psychic Conflict*. New York: International Universities Press.

Brenner, C. (1982). *The Mind in Conflict*. New York: International Universities Press.

Brierly, M. (1937). Affects in theory and practice. *International Journal of Psycho-Analysis, 18*: 256–268.

Brierly, M. (1951). Problems connected with the work of Melanie Klein. In: *Trends in Psycho-Analysis*. London: The Hogarth Press & The Institute of Psycho-Analysis.

Brodal, A. (1981). *Neurological Anatomy in Relation to Clinical Medicine* (3rd. ed.). New York: Oxford University Press.

Brome, V. (1967). *Freud and His Early Circle: The Struggles of Psycho-Analysis*. London: Heinemann.

Brook, A. (1994). *Kant and the Mind*. Cambridge: Cambridge University Press.

Burgner, M., & Edgcumbe, R. (1972a). Some problems in the conceptualization of early object relations: I. *Psychoanalytic Study of the Child, 27*: 283–314.

Burgner, M., & Edgcumbe, R. (1972b). Some problems in the conceptualization of early object relations: II. The concept of object constancy. *Psychoanalytic Study of the Child, 27*: 315–333.

Burlingham, D. T. (1952). *Twins: A Study of Three Pairs of Identical Twins*. London: Imago.

Burlingham, D. T. (1963). A study of identical twins – their analytic material compared with existing observation data of their early childhood. *Psychoanalytic Study of the Child, 18*: 367–423.

Changeux, J., & Connes, A. (1995). *Conversations on Mind, Matter and Mathematics*, transl. M. DeBevoise. Princeton, NJ: Princeton University Press.

Chapman, J., Freeman, T., & McGhie, A. (1950). Clinical research in schizophrenia—the psychotherapeutic approach. *British Journal of Medical Psychology, 32*: 75–85.

Couch, A. (1995). Anna Freud's adult psychoanalytic technique: a defence of classical analysis. *International Journal of Psycho-Analysis, 76*: 153–171.

Couch, A. (1997). "Extra-transference interpretation: a defence of classical technique." Paper presented to the Northern Ireland Association for the Study of Psycho-Analysis; a revised version of "Extra-transference interpretation: the debate continues", given to a Scientific Meeting of the British Psycho-Analytical Society on 1 November 1989.

Couch, A. (1999). Therapeutic functions of the real relationship in psychoanalysis. *Psychoanalytic Study of the Child, 54*: 130–168.

Crick, F. (1994). *The Astonishing Hypothesis: The Scientific Search for the Soul*. New York: Simon & Schuster.

Crick, F., & Koch, C. (1990). Towards a neurobiological theory of consciousness. *Seminars Neuroscience, 2*: 263–275.

Cuff, E. C., Sharrock, W. W., & Francis, D. W. (1998). *Perspectives in Sociology* (4th ed.). London: Routledge.

Dahl, H. (1979). The appetitive hypothesis of emotions: a new psychoanalytic model of motivation. In: C. Izard (Ed.), *Emotions in Personality and Psychopathology*. New York: Plenum.

Damasio, A. (1994). *Descartes' Error: Emotion, Reason, and the Human Brain*. New York: Putnam.

Damasio, A. (1999). *The Feeling of What Happens*, New York: Harcourt Brace.

Darwin, C. (1872). *The Expression of the Emotions in Man and Animals*. London.

Davie, J. M., & Freeman, T. (1961). Disturbances of perception and consciousness in schizophrenic states. *British Journal of Medical Psychology, 34*: 33–41.

Dennett, D. (1991). *Consciousness Explained*. Boston, MA: Little Brown.

Dostoevsky, F. (1880). *The Brothers Karamazov*, transl. R. Pevear & L. Volokhonsky. New York: Vintage, 1990.

Edelman, G. (1990). *The Remembered Present: A Biological Theory of Consciousness*. New York: Basic.

Edgcumbe, R. (1976). Some comments on the concept of the negative oedipal phase in girls. *Psychoanalytic Study of the Child, 31*: 35–61.

Edgcumbe, R., & Burgner, T. (1975). The phallic–narcissistic phase. *Psychoanalytic Study of the Child, 30*: 161–180.

Ekins, R., & Freeman, R. (Eds.) (1994). *Centres and Peripheries of Psychoanalysis*. London: Karnac Books.

Eliot, T. S. (1943). Burnt Norton. In: *Four Quartets*. New York: Harcourt.

Emde, R. (1988). Development terminable and interminable: innate and motivational factors. *International Journal of Psycho-Analysis*, 69: 23–42.

Erdelyi, M. E. (1985). *Psychoanalysis: Freud's Cognitive Psychology*. New York: W. H. Freeman.

Fairbairn, W. R. D. (1952). *Psychoanalytic Studies of the Personality*. London & New York: Tavistock/Routledge.

Felleman, D., & Van Essen, D. (1991). Distributed hierarchical processing in the primate cerebral cortex. *Cerebral Cortex, 1*: 1–47.

Ferenczi, S. (1913). Stages in the development of the sense of reality. In: *First Contributions to Psychoanalysis*, New York: Brunner/Mazel, 1980.

Fliess, R. (1961). *Ego and Body Ego*. New York: International Universities Press.

Freeman, R., & Freeman, T. (1992). An anatomical commentary on the concept of infantile oral sadism. *International Journal of Psychoanalysis, 73*: 343–348.

Freeman, T. (1969). *Psychopathology of the Psychoses*. London: Tavistock.

Freeman, T. (1988). *The Psychoanalyst in Psychiatry*. New Haven CT: Yale University Press.

Freeman, T. (1998). *But Facts Exist: An Enquiry into Psychoanalytic Theorizing*. London: Karnac Books.

Freeman, T., Cameron, J. L., & McGhie, A. (1958). *Chronic Schizophrenia*. New York: International Universities Press.

Freud, A. (1927). Introduction to the technique of child analysis. In: *The Writings of Anna Freud, Vol. 1*. New York: International Universities Press. (Under the title: *Four Lectures on Child Analysis*.)

Freud, A. (1936). *The Ego and the Mechanisms of Defence*. London: Hogarth Press.

Freud, A. (1962). Assessment of childhood pathology. *Psychoanalytic Study of the Child*, 17: 149–158.

Freud, A. (1974). A psychoanalytic view of developmental psychopathology. In: *The Writings of Anna Freud, Vol. 8.* New York: International Universities Press.

Freud, S. (1884e). On coca. In: *The Cocaine Papers*. New York: Stonehill.

Freud, S. (1885f). Addenda to "On coca". In: *The Cocaine Papers*. New York: Stonehill.

Freud, S. (1891b). *On Aphasia: A Critical Study*. New York: International Universities Press.

Freud, S. (1893a), with Breuer. On the psychical mechanism of hysterical phenomena: a lecture. *S.E.*, *3*.

Freud, S. (1893c). Some points for a comparative study of organic and hysterical motor paralyses. *S.E.*, *1*: 157.

Freud, S. (1894a). The neuro-psychoses of defence. *S.E.*, *3*: 157.

Freud, S. (1895c). Obsessions and phobias: their psychical mechanism and their aetiology. *S.E.*, *3*: 345.

Freud, S. (1895d). (with J. Breuer). *Studies on Hysteria. S.E.*, 2.

Freud, S. (1900a). *The Interpretation of Dreams. S.E.*, *4 & 5*.

Freud, S. (1901a). *On Dreams. S.E.*, 5: 633.

Freud, S. (1905c). Jokes and their relation to the unconscious. *S.E.*, *8*.

Freud, S. (1905d). Three essays on the theory of sexuality. *S.E.*, *7*: 125.

Freud, S. (1905e). Fragment of an analysis of a case of hysteria. *S.E.*, *7*: 3.

Freud, S. (1906a). My views on the part played by sexuality in the aetiology of the neuroses. *S.E.*, *7*: 271.

Freud, S. (1908b). Character and anal erotism. *S.E.*, *9*: 169.

Freud, S. (1909b). Analysis of a phobia in a five-year-old boy. *S.E. 10*: 3.

Freud, S. (1910h). A special type of object choice made by men. *S.E. 11*: 165.

Freud, S. (1912d). On the universal tendency to debasement in the sphere of love. *S.E.,11*: 179.

Freud, S. (1912–13). *Totem and Taboo. S.E.*, *13*: 1.

Freud,. S. (1913j). The claims of psycho-analysis to scientific interest. *S.E.*, *13*: 165.

Freud, S. (1914c). On narcissism: an introduction. *S.E.*, *14*: 69.

Freud, S. (1914g). Remembering, repeating and working through. Further recommendations on the technique of psycho-analysis, II. *S.E.*, *12*: 147.

Freud S. (1915c). Instincts and their vicissitudes. *S.E.*, *14*: 111.

Freud, S. (1915e). The unconscious. *S.E.*, *14*: 161.

Freud, S. (1916–17). *Introductory Lectures on Psycho-Analysis. S.E., 15–16.*

Freud, S. (1917d). A metapsychological supplement to the theory of dreams. *S.E., 14*: 222.

Freud, S. (1917e). Mourning and melancholia. *S.E., 14*: 239.

Freud, S. (1918a). The taboo of virginity. *S.E., 11*: 193.

Freud, S. (1920a). The psychogenesis of a case of female homosexuality. *S.E., 18*: 147.

Freud, S. (1920g). *Beyond the Pleasure Principle. S.E., 18*: 7.

Freud, S. (1921c). Group psychology and the analysis of the ego. *S.E., 18*: 69.

Freud, S. (1923b). *The Ego and the Id. S.E., 19*: 3.

Freud, S. (1924c). The economic problem of masochism. *S.E., 19*: 157.

Freud, S. (1925a). A note upon the "mystic writing-pad". *S.E., 19*: 227.

Freud, S. (1925e). The resistances to psycho-analysis. *S.E., 19*: 213.

Freud, S. (1925h). Negation. *S.E., 19*: 235.

Freud, S. (1926d). *Inhibitions, Symptoms and Anxiety. S.E., 20*: 77.

Freud, S. (1931b). Female sexuality. *S.E., 21*: 223.

Freud, S. (1933a). New Introductory Lectures on Psycho-Analysis. *S.E., 22*: 3.

Freud, S. (1937c). Analysis Terminable and Interminable. *S.E.*, 23.

Freud, S. (1939a). *Moses and Monotheism. S.E., 23*: 3.

Freud, S. (1940a). *An Outline of Psycho-Analysis. S.E., 23*: 141.

Freud, S. (1940b). Some elementary lessons in psycho-analysis. *S.E., 23*: 281.

Freud, S. (1950 [1892–1899]). Extracts from the Fliess Papers. *S.E., 1*: 177.

Freud, S. (1950 [1895]). A project for a scientific psychology. *S.E., 1*: 295.

Freud, S. (1950a [1887–1902]). *The Origins of Psycho-Analysis*. London: Imago.

Freud, S. (1994a). Letter to Einstein. In: I. Grubrich-Simitis, "No greater, richer, more mysterious subject [. . .] than the life of the mind." An early exchange of letters between Freud and Einstein. *International Journal of Psycho-Analysis, 76*: 115.

Freud, S., & Jones, E. (1993). *The Complete Correspondence of Sigmund Freud and Ernest Jones, 1908–1939*, ed. R. A. Paskauskas. Cambridge, MA, & London: Belknap Press.

Glassman, W. E. (1995). *Approaches to Psychology* (2nd ed.). Buckingham: Open University Press.

Glick, B. (1966). Freud, the problem of quality and the "secretory neuron". *Psychoanalytic Quarterly, 35*: 84.

Glover, E. (1945). Examination of the Klein System of Child Psychology. *Psychoanalytic Study of the Child, 1*: 75–118.

Groddeck, G. (1977). *The Meaning of Illness*. London: Hogarth & The Institute of Psycho-Analysis.

Grosskurth, P. (1991). *The Secret Ring: Freud's Inner Circle and the Politics of Psychoanalysis*. London: Jonathan Cape.

Hadley, J. (1992). The instincts revisited. *Psychoanalytic Inquiry, 12*: 396–418.

Hale, N. G., Jr. (1995). *The Rise and Crisis of Psychoanalysis in the United States: Freud and the Americans, 1917–1985*. New York: Oxford University Press.

Heimann, P. (1950). On counter-transference. *International Journal of Psycho-Analysis, 31*: 81.

Herzog, J. (1991). Temperament and transaction: constitutional, maturational and experiential components in character formation. *Bulletin of the Anna Freud Centre, 14*: 184–196,

Holt, R. (1965). A review of some of Freud's biological assumptions and their influence on his theories. In: *Psychoanalysis and Contemporary Thought*, ed. N. Greenfield & W. Lewis. Madison, WI, & Milwaukee: University of Wisconsin.

Holton, G. (1988). *The Thematic Origins of Scientific Thought*. Cambridge, MA: Harvard University Press.

Hoskins, R. (1936). An endocrine approach to psychodynamics. *Psychoanalytic Quarterly, 5*: 87–107.

Jackson, J. H. (1884). Evolution and dissolution of the nervous system. In: *Selected Writings of John Hughlings Jackson*. New York: Basic Books.

Jackson, J. H. (1887). An address on the psychology of joking. In: *Selected Writings of John Hughlings Jackson*. New York: Basic Books.

Jackson, J. H. (1894). The factors of insanities. In: *Selected Writings of John Hughlings Jackson*. New York: Basic Books.

Jacobson, E. (1953). The affects and their pleasure–unpleasure qualities in relation to the psychic discharge process. In: R. Loewenstein (Ed.), *Drives, Affects, Behavior, 1*. New York: International Universities Press.

Jacoby, L. (1984). Incidental vs. intentional retrieval: remembering and awareness as separate issues. In: L. Squires & N. Butters (Eds.), *The Neuropsychology of Memory*. New York: Guildford.

James, H. (1948 [1996]). *The Other House*. London: Rupert Hart-Davis.

Jones, E. (1955). The God complex. In: *Essays in Applied Psychoanalysis*. New York: International Universities Press.

Jones, E. (1953–57). *Sigmund Freud: Life and Work*. London: Hogarth.

Kant, I. (1781). *Critique of Pure Reason,* transl. N. Kemp-Smith. New York: St. Martins Press, 1929.

Kaplan-Solms, K., & Solms, M. (2000). *Clinical Studies in Neuro-Psychoanalysis: An Introduction to Depth Neuropsychology. Journal of the American Psychoanalytic Association Monograph Series, 5.* London: Karnac Books; Madison, CT: International Universities Press.

Kernberg, O. (1975). *Borderline Conditions and Pathological Narcissism.* New York: Jason Aronson.

Kernberg, O. (1988). Psychic structure and structural change: an ego psychology—object relations theory viewpoint. *Journal of the American Psychoanalytic Association, 36*: 315–338.

Kernberg, O. (1992). The psychopathology of hatred. In: T. Shapiro & R. Emde (Eds.), *Affect: Psychoanalytic Perspectives.* Madison, CT: International Universities Press.

King, P., & Steiner, R. Eds. (1995). *The Freud–Klein Controversies, 1941–45.* London: Tavistock/Routledge.

Krutch, J. W. (1926). *Edgar Allan Poe: A Study in Genius.* New York: Alfred A. Knopf.

Kutter, P. (1992). *Psychoanalysis International: A Guide to Psychoanalysis throughout the World. Volume 1: Europe.* Stuttgart–Bad Canstatt: Frommann-Holzboog.

Kutter, P. (1995). *Psychoanalysis International: A Guide to Psychoanalysis throughout the World. Volume 2: America, Asia, Australia, Further European Countries.* Stuttgart–Bad Canstatt: Frommann-Holzboog.

Lacan, J. (1966). Le seminaire sur "La Lettre volée". In: *Écrits.* Paris: Editions du Seuil.

Lampl-de-Groot, J. (1980). Flashes of memory: on the development of psychoanalysis and the "psychoanalytic movement" especially in the twenties and thirties. In: *Man and Mind: Collected Papers of Jeanne Lampl-de Groot.* New York: International Universities Press, 1985.

Laplanche, J., & Pontalis, J-B. (1973). *The Language of Psycho-Analysis.* London: Karnac Books, 1988.

Laufer, M. E. (1994). Formulation of interpretation: from truth to experience. *International Journal of Psycho-Analysis, 75*: 1093–1105.

Leupold-Löwenthal, H. (1992). Austria: the Viennese Psychoanalytic Society from 1918 to 1945. In: P. Kutter, (Ed.), *Psychoanalysis International: A Guide to Psychoanalysis Throughout the World. Volume 1: Europe.* Stuttgart-Bad Canstatt: Frommann-Holzboog.

Lewin, B. (1965). Reflections on affect. In: M. Schur (Ed.), *Drives, Affects, Behavior,* 2. New York: International Universities Press.

Lewis, P. W. (1930). *The Apes of God.* London: The Arthur Press. [Reprinted 1981, with an afterword by Paul Edwards. Santa Barbara, CA: Black Sparrow Press.]

Libet, B. (1985). Unconscious cerebral initiative and the role of conscious will in voluntary action. *Behavioral and Brain Sciences, 8*: 529–566.

Lichtenberg, J. (1988). A theory of motivational–functional systems as psychic structures. *Journal of the American Psychoanalytic Association, 36*: 57–72.

Lichtenberg, J. (1989). *Psychoanalysis and Motivation,* Hillsdale, NJ: Erlbaum.

Loewald, H. (1960). On the therapeutic action of psychoanalysis. In: *Papers on Psychoanalysis* (pp. 221–256). New Haven, CT: Yale University Press, 1980.

Loewald, H. (1966). Book review: *Psychoanalytic Concepts and the Structural Theory,* by J. Arlow & C. Brenner. In: *Papers on Psychoanalysis.* New Haven, CT: Yale University Press, 1980.

Mahler, M., Bergman, A., & Pine, F. (1975). *The Psychological Birth of the Human Infant,* New York: Basic Books.

Mandler, J. (1990). A new perspective on cognitive development in infancy. *American Scientist, 78*: 236–243.

Marcel, A. (1883). Conscious and unconscious perception. *Cognitive Psychology, 15*: 238–300.

Marcel, A. (1988). Phenomenal experience and functionalism. In: A. Marcel & E. Bisiach (Eds.), *Consciousness in Contemporary Science.* Oxford: Clarendon.

McCarley, R., & Hobson, J. (1977). The neurobiological origins of psychoanalytic dream theory. *American Journal of Psychiatry, 134*: 1211.

McGuire, W. (1974). *The Freud/Jung Letters: The Correspondence between Sigmund Freud and C. G. Jung.* London: Hogarth and Routledge & Kegan Paul.

McLean, D. (1992). Maturational and experiential components in character formation. *Psychoanalytic Study of the Child, 47*: 235–252. [Summary in: *Bulletin of the Anna Freud Centre, 14* (1991): 164–171.]

Merikle, P. (1992). Perception without awareness. *American Psychologist* (June 1992): 792–795.

Merikle, P., & Joordens, S. (1996). Measuring unconscious influences. In: *Scientific Approaches to the Question of Consciousness,* ed. J. Coven & J. Scholar. Mahwah, NJ: Erlbaum.

Mesulam, M.-M. (1985). Patterns in behavioral neuroanatomy: association areas, the limbic system, and hemispheric specialization.

In: Mesulam, M.-M. (Ed.), *Principles of Behavioural Neurology*. Philadelphia, PA: F. A. Davis.

Muhlleitner, E., & Reichmayr, J. (1997). Following Freud in Vienna: the Psychological Wednesday Society and the Viennese Psycho-Analytical Society 1902–1938. *International Forum for Psychoanalysis, 6*: 73–102.

Muller, J. P., & Richardson, W. J. (Eds.) (1988). *The Purloined Poe. Lacan, Derrida and Psychoanalytic Reading*. Baltimore, MD, & London: The Johns Hopkins University Press.

Myers, J. (1992). *Edgar Allan Poe: His Life and Legacy*. London: John Murray.

Nagel, T. (1974). What is it like to be a bat? In: *Mortal Questions*. New York: Cambridge University Press, 1979.

Noy, P. (1977). Metapsychology as a multimodel system. *International Review of Psycho-Analysis, 4*: 1–12.

Nunberg, H. (1931). The synthetic function of the ego. *International Journal of Psycho-Analysis, 12*: 123–140.

Opatow, B. (1988). The self as desire: a Freudian dialectic. *Psychoanalysis and Contemporary Thought, 11*: 613–637.

Opatow, B. (1989). Drive theory and the metapsychology of experience. *International Journal of Psycho-Analysis, 70*: 645–660.

Opatow, B. (1993). On the drive-rootedness of psychoanalytic ego psychology. *International Journal of Psycho-Analysis, 74*: 437–457.

Ostrom, J. W. (Ed.) (1966). *The Letters of Edgar Allan Poe*, 2 vols. New York: Gordian Press.

Panksepp, J. (1985). Mood disorders. In: P. Vinken, G. Bruyn, H. Klawans, & J. Fredericks (Eds.), *Handbook of Clinical Neurology, 45*.

Panksepp, J. (1998). *Affective Neuroscience*. Oxford: Oxford University Press.

Payne, R. W. (1961). Cognitive abnormalities. In: *Handbook of Abnormal Psychology*, ed. H. Eysenck. New York: Basic Books.

Pylyshyn, Z. (1989). Computing in cognitive science. In: *Foundations of Cognitive Science*, ed. M. Posner (pp. 49–92). Cambridge: M.I.T. Press.

Quinn, A. H. (1941). *Edgar Allan Poe: A Critical Biography*. New York: Appleton-Century.

Rapaport, D. (1951). *Organisation and Pathology of Thought: Selected Sources*. New York: Columbia University Press.

Rapaport, D. (1953). On the psycho-analytic theory of affects. *International Journal of Psycho-Analysis*, 34: 177–198.

Rapaport, D. (1960). *The Structure of Psychoanalytic Theory*. Psychological Issues Monograph 6. New York: International Universities Press.

Reich, W. (1928). On character analysis. In: *The Psychoanalytic Reader*, ed. R. Fliess. London: Hogarth Press, 1950.

Richards, A. (1998). Arnold D. Richards, M.D. In: A. Richards, E. Nersessian, J. Ennis, & K. Calder, "The 'common ground' of psychoanalysis." In: M. Furer, E. Nersessian, & C. Perri (Eds.), *Controversies in Contemporary Psychoanalysis: Lectures from the New York Psychoanalytic Institute*. Madison, CT: International Universities Press.

Ricoeur, P. (1970). *Freud and Philosophy*, transl. D. Savage. New Haven, CT: Yale University Press.

Rothman, S. M. (1995). *Living in the Shadow of Death: Tuberculosis and the Social Experience of Illness in American History*. Baltimore, MD, & London: The Johns Hopkins University Press.

Roustang, F. (1986). *Lacan de l'Equivoque à l'Impasse*. Paris: Editions de Minuit.

Sandler, J. (1972). The role of affects in psychoanalytic theory. In: *From Safety to Superego*. London: Karnac Books.

Sandler, J. (1988). The child that is in man. In: W. A. Koelsch & S. Wagner (Eds.), *Freud in Our Time: A Seventy-Fifth Anniversary Symposium*. Worcester, MA: Clark University Press.

Sandler J., with A. Freud (1985). *The Analysis of Defense*. New York: International Universities Press.

Schafer, R. (1976). *Tradition and Change in Psychoanalysis*. London: Karnac Books, 1997.

Schilder, P. (1953). *Medical Psychology*. New York: International Universities Press.

Schlesinger, H. (1991). What does psychoanalysis have to contribute to the understanding of character? *Bulletin of the Anna Freud Centre, 14*: 155–163.

Schore, A. (1994). *Affect Regulation and the Origin of the Self: The Neurobiology of Emotional Development*. Hillsdale, NJ: Erlbaum.

Schwartz, A. (1988). Reification revisited: some neurologically filtered views of psychic structure and conflict. *Journal of the American Psychoanalytic Association, 36*: 359–385.

Searle, J. (1980). Minds, brains and programs. *Behavioral and Brain Sciences, 3*: 417–424.

Searle, J. (1983). *Intentionality: An Essay on the Philosophy or Mind*. New York: Cambridge University Press.

Shengold, L. (1989). Everything: a poetic meditation on Freud's question: "what does a woman want?" *International Journal of Psycho-Analysis, 70*: 419–422.

Shengold, L. (1991a). Contribution to first plenary discussion, Twelfth International Scientific Colloquium, Anna Freud Centre. *Bulletin of the Anna Freud Centre, 14*: 183.

Shengold, L. (1991b). *"Father: Don't You See I'm Burning?"* New Haven, CT: Yale University Press.

Shengold, L. (1993). *"The Boy Will Come to Nothing!": Freud's Ego Ideal and Freud as Ego Ideal.* New Haven, CT: Yale University Press.

Shevrin, H. (1992). Subliminal perception, memory, and consciousness: cognitive and dynamic perspectives. In: *Perception without Awareness,* ed. R. Bornstein & T. Pittman (pp. 123–148). New York: Guilford Press.

Shevrin, H., Bond, J., Brakel, L., Hertel R., & Williams, W. (1996). Cognitive theory. In: *Conscious and Unconscious Processes: Psychodynamic, Cognitive and Neuropsychological Convergences.* New York: Guilford Press.

Silverman, K. (1991). *Edgar A. Poe: Mournful and Never-ending Remembrance.* New York: HarperCollins.

Solms, M. (1995a). Is the brain more real than the mind? *Psychoanalytic Psychotherapy, 9*: 107–120.

Solms, M. (1995b). New findings on the neurological organization of dreaming: implications for psychoanalysis. *Psychoanalytic Quarterly, 64*: 43–67.

Solms, M. (1996). Towards an anatomy of the unconscious. *Journal of Clinical Psychoanalysis, 5*: 331–367.

Solms, M. (1997a). *The Neuropsychology of Dreams: A Clinico–Anatomical Study.* Mahwah, NJ: Erlbaum.

Solms, M. (1997b). Review of A. Damasio (1994): *Descartes' Error: Emotion, Reason, and the Human Brain. Journal of the American Psychoanalytic Association, 45*: 959–964.

Solms, M. (1997c). Review of A. Schore (1994): *Affect regulation and the origin of the self: the neurobiology of emotional development. Journal of the American Psychoanalytic Association, 45*: 964–969.

Solms, M. (1997d). What is consciousness? *Journal of the American Psychoanalytic Association, 45*: 681–703.

Solms, M. (2000). Dreaming and REM sleep are controlled by different brain mechanisms. *Behavioral and Brain Science, 23* (6).

Solms, M., & Nersessian, E. (1999). Freud's theory of affect: questions for neuroscience. *Neuro-Psychoanalysis, 1*: 5–14.

Solms, M., & Saling, M. (1986). On psychoanalysis and neuroscience:

Freud's attitude to the localizationist tradition. *International Journal of Psycho-Analysis, 67*: 397–416.

Solnit, A. J. (1988). Foreword. In: T. Freeman, *The Psychoanalyst in Psychiatry*. New Haven, CT: Yale University Press.

Solnit, A. J. (1991). Contribution to first plenary discussion, Twelfth International Scientific Colloquium, Anna Freud Centre. *Bulletin of the Anna Freud Centre, 14*: 180–181.

Spelke, E. (1988). The origins of physical knowledge. In: *Thought without Language*, ed. L. Weiskrantz. Oxford: Oxford University Press.

Sterba, R. F. (1934). The fate of the ego in psychoanalytic therapy. *International Journal of Psycho-Analysis*: 117–126.

Sterba, R. F. (1982). *Reminiscences of a Viennese Psychoanalyst*. Detroit, MI: Wayne State University Press.

Stern, D. (1985). *The Interpersonal World of the Infant*. New York: Basic Books.

Stern, D. (1990). Joy and satisfaction in infancy. In: R. Glick & S. Bone (Eds.), *Pleasure Beyond the Pleasure Principle*. New Haven, CT: Yale University Press.

Tartakoff, H. H. (1966). The normal personality in our culture and the Nobel Prize complex. In: R. M. Loewenstein, L. M. Newman, M. Schur, e. al. (Eds.), *Psychoanalysis: A General Psychology. Essays in Honor of Heinz Hartmann*. New York: International Universities Press.

Turkle, S. (1979). *Psychoanalytic Politics: Jacques Lacan and Freud's French Revolution*. London: Burnett Books.

Tyson, P. (1998). The psychology of women, continued. *Journal of the American Psychoanalytic Association, 46*: 361–363.

Valenstein, A. (1958). Panel report: the psychoanalytic concept of character. *Journal of the American Psychoanalytic Association, 6*: 567–575.

Valenstein, A. (1991). Contribution to first plenary discussion. Twelfth International Scientific Colloquium. *Bulletin of the Anna Freud Centre, 14*: 182–183.

Von Domarus, E. (1944). The specific laws of logic in schizophrenia. In: *Language and Thought in Schizophrenia*, ed. J. S. Kasanin. New York: Norton, 1964.

Waelder, R. (1936). The principle of multiple function. *Psychoanalytic Quarterly, 5*: 45–62.

Waelder, R. (1937). The problem of the genesis of psychical conflict in earliest infancy. *International Journal of Psycho-Analysis, 18*: 406–473.

Waelder, R. (1960). *Basic Theory of Psychoanalysis*. New York: International Universities Press.

Wallerstein, R. (1988). One psychoanalysis or many? *International Journal of Psychoanalysis, 69*: 5–21.

Wallerstein, R. (1991). Final summarising statement of proceedings at the Twelfth International Scientific Colloquium, Anna Freud Centre. *Bulletin of the Anna Freud Centre, 14*: 233–250.

Wallerstein, R. S. (1992). One Psychoanalysis or Many? In: R. S. Wallerstein (Ed.), *The Common Ground of Psychoanalysis*. North Vale, NJ: Jason Aronson.

Wallerstein, R. S. (1995). Reality. In: B. E. Moore & B. D. Fines (Eds.), *Psychoanalysis: The Major Concepts*. New Haven, CT: Yale University Press.

Werner, H. (1957). *Comparative Psychology of Mental Development*. New York: International Universities Press.

Winnicott, D. W. (1957). Stealing and telling lies. In: *The Child and the Family: First Relationships*. London: Tavistock.

Winnicott, D. W. (1964). *The Family and Individual Development*. London: Tavistock.

Yorke, C. (1971). Some suggestions for a critique of Kleinian psychology. *Psychoanalytic Study of the Child, 26*: 129–155.

Yorke, C. (1983). Clinical notes on developmental pathology. *Psychoanalytic Study of the Child, 38*: 389–402.

Yorke, C. (1986). Reflections on the problem of psychic trauma. *Psychoanalytic Study of the Child, 41*: 221–236.

Yorke, C. (1991). Freud's "On Narcissism": a teaching text. In: J. J. Sandler, P. Fonagy, & E. S. Person (Eds.), *Freud's "On Narcissism: An Introduction"*. New Haven, CT: Yale University Press.

Yorke, C. (1992). Foreword. In: E. E. Garcia (Ed.), *Understanding Freud: The Man and His Ideas*. New York: New York University Press.

Yorke, C. (1994). Freud or Klein: conflict or compromise. *International Journal of Psycho-Analysis, 75*: 375–385.

Yorke, C. (1995). Freud's psychology: can it survive? *Psychoanalytic Study of the Child, 50*: 3–31.

Yorke, C. (1998). Openness and rigidity. *Institute of Psychoanalysis News* (Autumn).

Yorke, C., Wiseberg, S., & Freeman, T. (1989). *Development and Psychopathology: Studies in Psychoanalytic Psychiatry*. New Haven, CT: Yale University Press.

Young-Bruehl, E. (1988). *Anna Freud: A Biography*. New York: Summit Books.

Zeki, S. (1993). *A Vision of the Brain*. Oxford: Blackwell.

INDEX

Abend, S. M., 96
Abraham, K., 6, 125, 130
Abrams, S., 97, 102–107
addiction, 106
  treatment of, 79
Adler, A., 2
affect(s), 45–81
  anatomy and physiology of, 62–78
  as arising from within, 54–57
  mechanism of, 54, 61
    subjective, 54
  metapsychology of, 13, 63, 77
  as primary sensory modality, 12, 56–59
  projected, 55
  psychic manifestations of, 54, 56
    and physical manifestations, 45–49
  and schizophrenias, 92
  somatic manifestations of, 48, 55, 56
  "taming" of, 63
  theory, 17, 47, 61
    Freud's, 12, 45–46, 59, 60–61, 78, 100
  see also James–Lange theory of emotion
aggression, 75, 101, 111
  as drive, 5, 9
Aguayo, J., 5–7
Allan, J., 16, 120–122, 129
Amacher, P., 78
anal sadistic phase, 112, 126
Anna Freud Centre, 13, 95, 107
anti-essentialism, 9
anxiety:
  location of source of, 80
  pharmacological control of, 47
  somatic symptoms of, 47
  transformation theory of [Freud], 5
Arlow, J., 27
attachment, 76, 108, 112, 113, 122
attention, mechanism of, 69

Bailie, R., ix, xiii, 16–17, 119–136
Bass, A., 19
Baudelaire, C., 119, 122
Baudry, F., 96, 100–102, 104
benzodiazepines, 47
Bergman, A., 3

B Group (Contemporary Freudian Group), 2
Bibring, E., 4, 6
Bibring, G., 6
Bion, W. R., 49
  bizarre objects, 54
  theory of pre-conception of, 57
Bionian perspective, 3
Bird, B., 27
bisexuality, 110, 113
bizarre objects [Bion], 54
Bleuler, E., 88
Bohr, N., 25
Bonaparte, M., 7, 119, 120
Bond, J., 10
brain syndrome, chronic, 14, 85, 87, 88
Brakel, L., 10
breast, wishful hallucination of, 55
Brenner, C., 28, 31, 46, 57, 59
Brierly, M., 59, 61
British Kleinianism, 3
British Psychoanalytical Society, 4, 7
Brodal, A., 65, 67, 70, 73
Brome, V., 2
Brook, A., 49
Brücke, E. W. von, 52
Burgner, M., 114
Burgner, T., 109, 114
Burlingham, D. T., 7, 13, 14, 97
butyrophenones, 47
Buxbaum, E., 4

Cameron, J. L., 85
castration anxiety, 8, 102
censorship, 93
cerebrum:
  inner surface of, 70–78
  outer surface of, 65–70
Changeux, J., 40
Chapman, J., 87
character:
  analysis, 101
  definition of, 103–104
  formation, 97
    and drives, 99
    and sexual identity, 107, 109
  Freud's theory on, 100–102
  metapsychology of, 16, 99
  neurosis(es), 96, 97
  organization, 104
  psychoanalytic study of, 15, 95–118
  and sexual identity, 109–115
  structure, 15
    rigid, 117
  trait(s), 99, 105, 115, 118
    changes in, in adolescence, 104
    and character structure, differentiation of, 15, 104
    continuity of, 103–106
    and drives, 100
    maladaptive, 96
    pathological, 103
Chiland, C., 107
child:
  analysis, 7, 14, 15
  development, 96
  infant observation, 96, 97
chronic brain syndrome, 14, 85–88
Claverhouse, Graham of, 91
Clemm, M., 122, 123, 127, 131, 132
cognition:
  pathological forms of, 13, 14, 83–94
    and dream thoughts, 89–92
cognitive organizations, Rapaport's concept of, 92
cognitive psychology, 11, 12, 19, 21, 34, 96
composition, Freud's concept of, 91–92
compromise formation, 29–31, 36, 97
condensation, 93, 94
  archaic (pre-logical) means of, 93
conflict:
  external, 15
  internal, 15
    and character, 107–109
  internalized, 15
  theory, 29
  types of, 107
Connes, A., 40
consciousness, 29–33, 35–42, 44, 67, 68, 72–79, 93
  and compromise formation, 29, 31
  ego, 36
  empirical, 35, 36
    and psychic reality, 34
    repression of, 38
  envelope of, 12, 57, 58
  external surface of, 52, 54, 56, 59, 62, 63
  Freud on, 50–52
  hallucinatory, 35

internal surface of, 12, 49, 52, 54, 56, 59, 62, 81
introspective, 12
and memory(ies), 24
mentality under, 41–42
mode of, psychoanalytic unconscious as, 35, 37
and motivation, 33
negativity of, 40
and perceptions, 12
and psychic pain, 35
repressed, 33
and repudiation and negation, 33
and secondary process, 33
theory of, 10, 11, 17, 20, 37
and dreams, 23
Freud's, 19–20, 22
and unconscious wish, 25, 28, 29
Contemporary Freudian ("B") Group, 2
cortex, 65, 68–77
units of, 65
Couch, A., 4, 7–9
countertransference, 80
Crick, F., 68
Cuff, E. C., 1

Dahl, H., 46
Damasio, A., 48, 56, 70, 73, 77, 80
Darwin, C., 47
Davie, J. M., 87
defence(s), 8, 15, 38, 93, 126, 129, 133, 136
-drive conflicts, 28–29, 31
mechanisms, 102, 117
denial, 117
projection, 128
delusion(s), 131
delusional reality, 14, 17, 84, 89
Dennett, D., 80
depression, pharmacological control of, 47
depth psychology, 10
desire, and knowledge, 33–44
Deutsch, H., 4, 6
developmental reconstructions, 8
dibenzodiazepines, 47
displacement, 94
archaic (pre-logical) means of, 93
Dostoevsky, F., 39, 128
dream(s), 13, 16, 76, 92
essence of, 22
Freud's theory of, 8, 9, 21–26, 89
thoughts, and cognition, 89–93
and wish-fulfilment, 21–32
-work, 16, 22, 26, 43, 89
drive(s), 29, 31, 43, 44, 46, 80, 130
aggression as, 9
[Freud], 5
and character formation, 99
-defence conflicts, 28–29, 31
derivatives, 15, 28, 31, 102
sexual, 20
endogenous, 78
Freud's theory of, 46, 51, 100–102
infantile, 25
organization, 15, 101
theory, vs. affect theory, 46
drugs, psychopharmacological action of, 47
Duncan, J., 4
dynamic–economic theory of mental life [Freud], 3, 4, 10
dynamic point of view, 8
dynamic unconscious, 29, 35, 36, 38
discovery of, 23
psychic reality of, 11, 26

economic point of view, 8
Edelman, G., 68
Edgcumbe, R., 109, 114
ego, 3, 44, 57, 61, 97
bodily, 70, 80
consciousness, 36
defences, 9
development, 8–9, 15, 30, 38, 101
distortion, 102
emotional, 80
functioning, 99, 117
-ideal, 101
–id–superego:
relationship, 15
structure, 9
mastery, 16
primitive, 126
psychogenesis of, 35
psychology, 2–3, 16
structural, 2, 65–69, 73, 77
structure, 30
transcendental, 30, 36
Einstein, A., 21
Eissler, K., 20

Ekins, R., ix, xi, xii, 1–17
Eliot, T. S., 43
Emde, R., 46
emotion, James–Lange theory of, 56, 73
empathy [*Einfühlung*], 80
  mechanism of, 54
envy, 57, 114
Erdelyi, M. E., 10
external reality, 9

Fairbairn, W. R. D., 4, 126
fantasy:
  and hallucination, 21–32
  infantile, 25
  oral sadistic, 130, 136
  unconscious, 21, 26, 27, 33, 44, 130
    efficacy of, 27
    mechanisms of, 11, 27–32
    psychic reality of, 31
  see also phantasy
Federn, P., 4
Felleman, D., 69
femininity, and character, 109
Ferenczi, S., 6, 36, 37
Flanagan, O., 19
Fliess, R., 121
Fliess, W., 23
Fogel, G., 19
Francis, D. W., 1
Freeman, R., xii, 4, 125, 130
Freeman, T., ix–x, xii, xiii, 4, 13–14, 17, 83–94, 96, 97, 130
Freud, A., xii, xiii, 4–9, 13–15, 107, 114
  Freud–Klein Controversies, 2
Freud, S. *(passim)*
  affect theory of, 12, 45–46, 59–61, 78, 100
  on aggression as drive, 5
  on character, 100–102
  classical psychoanalysis of, xi–xiii
  concept:
    of character of, 100
    of composition of, 91–92
  conceptualizations of reality of, 9
  on condensation, 93
  on consciousness, 50–51
  on distinction between sexes, 110–115
  on dream(s):
    thoughts, 89–92
    theory, 9, 22–32
  drive theory of, 46, 51, 100–102
  dynamic–economic theory of mental life of, 3
  electi of, 5, 7
  on envy, 114
  exclusion of dissenters by, 1–2
  on formal regression, 93
  on identification, 101
  inner circle of, 4–6
  Kinderseminar, 6
  libido theory, 125
  "Little Hans", 114
  metapsychology of, 8–11, 17, 22, 23, 61, 73
    vs. model of mind of, 60
  model of mind of, 60
  on narcissism:
    of beautiful women, 112
    of hypochondriasis, 106
    in puberty, 112
  neurones, ϕ system of, 65
  on object choice found in men, 101
  on primary process, 13
  "Q screens", 65
  on repetition compulsion, 101
  on resistance in analysis, 101
  secret committee of, 5
  signal theory, 5
  structural model of mind of, 2–5, 8–9, 20, 33
  theory:
    of anxiety, 5
    of mind as apparatus, 34
    of mobile cathexes, 94
    of the unconscious, 20–44
  topographical model, 2, 20
  transformation theory of anxiety of, 5

Galt, W., 121
gender identity, 114
Glassman, W. E., 1
Glick, B., 71
Glover, E., 2
Griswold, R., 119
Groddeck, G., 52
Grosskurth, P., 2, 5
Grossman, W. I., 19

Hadley, J., 78
Hale, N. G., Jr., 2
hallucination(s), 24, 131
  and fantasy, 21–32
  infantile, 25–26
  metapsychological, 30
  vs. perception, 30, 31, 41
  wishful, 30
Hartmann, H., xii, 2–4
Heimann, P., 80
Helmholtz, H. L. F. von, 52
heredity, 97
Hertel R., 10
Herzog, J., 103
Hobson, J., 78
Hoffer, W., 4, 8, 14
Holland, N., 120
Holt, R., 78
Holton, G., 21
Hoskins, R., 71
hypochondriasis:
  monosymptomatic, 106
  narcissism of, 106
hypothalamus, 70, 71, 73
hysteria, 23, 80

id, 97, 99
  –ego–superego:
    relationship, 15
    structure, 9
  psychogenesis of, 35
identification, 38, 90–91, 101–102, 108, 110
  and ego development, 101
  feminine, 114
  predicative, 43
identity:
  gender, 114
  sense of, 113
  sexual: *see* sexual identity
illusion, 30, 31
  transference, 44
    perceptual, 43
  Winnicott's notion of, 30
incorporation, 125
Independent (Middle) Group, 2
infantile amnesia, 9, 117
infantile sexuality, 9, 26
infant observation, 96, 97
instinct, transformation of, 16
instinctual drives, 9
interactionist perspective, 1
International Psychoanalytical Association (IPA), 2
interpersonal perspective, 3
interpretation, 8, 22, 79, 80
intersubjective perspective, 3

Jackson, J. H., 92, 99
Jacobson, E., 59
Jacoby, L., 77
James, H., 95, 118
James–Lange theory of emotion/affect, 56, 73
Jones, E., 4, 6, 115
Joordens, S., 25, 33
Joyce, J., 31
Jung, C. G., 2, 57

Kant, I., 30, 36, 37, 49, 51–53, 55
Kaplan-Solms, K., 77, 78
Kernberg, O., 3, 46
Kinderseminar, 6
King, P., 2
Kite, J., 19
Klein, M., 2, 4–7, 36
  Freud–Klein Controversies, 2
Kleinian Group, 2, 3
Kleinian perspective, 2–3, 10, 79
kleptomania, 130
knowledge and desire, 33–44
Kris, E., xii, 4, 20
Kris, T., 107
Krutch, J. W., 120–123, 128, 131, 133
Kutter, P., 2

Lacan, J., 120,
Lacanian perspective, 3, 10, 120
Lampl-de-Groot, J., 4, 7
Laplanche, J., 59
Laufer, M. E., 80
Leupold-Löwenthal, H., 4, 5, 7
Lewin, B., 59
Lewis, P. W., 107
Libet, B., 19, 33
libido, Freud's theory of, 125
Lichtenberg, J., 46
lithium, 47
"Little Hans", Freud's case of, 114
Loewald, H., 20, 27

London Institute of Psychoanalysis, 2, 13
Longfellow, H. W., 128

Mack-Brunswick, R., 7
Mahler, M., 3
Mandler, J., 40
maniacal psychoses, 13, 83
manic episodes, pharmacological control of, 47
Marcel, A., 33, 49
masculinity and character, 109
masochism, 112
Maxwell, J. C., 21
McCarley, R., 78
McGhie, A., 85, 87
McGuire, W., 57
McLean, D., 98, 100, 103
memory(ies), 8, 38, 120
  acting out in place of, 101
  and discharge of neurones, 72
  disorder, 13, 92, 117, 125
    in schizophrenias, 13, 88–89
  episodic, 76–77
  vs. perception, 24
  structural influence of, 60
  syncretic, 43
  traces, 68, 76–77
Merikle, P., 19, 25, 33, 35
Mesulam, M.-M., 64–73
Middle (Independent) Group, 2
mind:
  as apparatus, 34
  psycho-physical theory of, 9
mobile cathexes, Freud's theory of, 94
monoamine oxidase inhibitors, 47
Moss, D., 19
mother–infant relationship, impact of, 9
Muhlleitner, E., 4, 5
Muller, J. P., 120, 134
Müller, J., 52
Myers, J., 119, 128

Nagel, T., 25
narcissism:
  of beautiful women, 112
  extreme, of monosymptomatic hypochondriasis, 106
  of hypochondriasis, 106
  infantile, 112
  and object love, 8, 113
  of old age, 107
  in puberty, 112
negation, 31, 33, 40
  logical, 39
  psychoanalytic concept of, 39
  and reality testing, 24
  significance of, 39
Nersessian, E., 59, 100
neurasthenia, 80
neuroscience, 11, 12, 19, 33
neurosis(es), 102
  character, 96–97
  hysterical, 48
  symptom, 96–97
Northern Ireland Association for the Study of Psychoanalysis, 13
Noy, P., 8
Nunberg, H., xii, 4, 6

object relations:
  internal, 20
  theory, 2–3
oedipal phase, 97, 102, 109, 112
  female negative, 114
Oedipus complex, 2, 8, 100–102, 110, 117
ontogenesis, 24, 26
Opatow, B., x, xiii, 10–11, 13, 16, 19–44
openness and rigidity, and character structure, 15, 115–118
oral phase, 16, 125–126
oral–sadistic phase, 122, 126
Ostrom, J. W., 122, 131

panic attacks, pharmacological control of, 47
Panksepp, J., 48, 74, 75
paranoid delusions, 106
Payne, R. W., 92
penis envy, 108, 113, 114
perception:
  conscious, 51, 55, 68
  cross-modal, 36
  external, 11, 50, 52, 53, 56, 76
  vs. hallucination, 30, 31, 41
  internal, 53, 56, 58, 76, 79
    vs. external, 50, 56

vs. memory, 24
objective, 38, 55
ego's capacity for, 30
physical, 12
vs. psychic perception, 49
psychic, 12, 49, 56, 78, 79
secondary process, 30
sensory, 50, 58
subjective, 54
subliminal, 33
unconscious, 33
visual, 69, 78
perceptual anomalies, 13
in schizophrenias, 87
perceptual constancy, loss of, 87
perceptual identity, 41
perseveration, 13, 84
perversions, sexual, 112
phallic phase, 108, 112–113
–narcissistic, 114
–oedipal, 114
phantasy(ies)
unconscious, 60
[Kleinian], 79
phase:
anal sadistic, 112, 126
oedipal, 97, 102, 109, 112
female negative, 114
oral, 16, 125, 126
sadistic, 125, 126
phallic, 108, 112, 113
–narcissistic, 114
–oedipal, 114
phenomenological philosophy, 12
phenothiazines, 47
Piaget, J., 40
Pine, F., 3
pituitary gland, 71
plagiarism complex, 130
pleasure, 56–60, 73–77
and affect, 13
and hallucinated satisfaction, 42
-lust centre, 75, 76
and primary process, 42
principle, 9, 35, 79
pursuit of, and affects, 46, 57
Poe, Elizabeth, 120, 125, 126
Poe, Edgar Allan, 16, 119–136
"Berenice", 123–127, 130
"The Cask of Amontillado", 130
"The Fall of the House of Usher", 130
"The Purloined Letter", 120, 127, 130, 132–136
"William Wilson", 125
Poe, V. [née Clemm], 123–124, 127
Pontalis, J.-B., 59
positivist perspective, 1
post-ego psychological perspective, 3
post-structural perspective, 1
pre-conception, Bion's theory of, 57
predicative identification, 43
primary process, 11, 26, 37, 41–44, 63, 93, 94
[Freud], 13
functioning, 29–30, 38
repression of, 41
syntax of, 42
thinking, 14
vs. secondary-process thinking, 9, 29–30
transformations, 22, 43
and unconscious wishes, 21
primary sensory modality, affect as, 12, 56, 58, 59
Principle of Multiple Function, 99
processing, conscious vs. unconscious, 33
projection:
defence of, 128
pathological, 54, 79
psychic dissolution, 14, 88, 93
psychoanalysis:
developmental theory of, 36
Lacanian: *see* Lacanian psychoanalysis
metapsychologies within, 1
as social psychology, 1
psychoanalytic unconscious, distinctiveness of, 19–44
psychogenetic point of view, 8
psychopharmacology, 46, 46–47, 79
psycho-physical theory of mind, 9
psychosis, amphetamine, 106
psychosomatic conditions, treatment of, 79
Pylyshyn, Z., 43

"Q screens" [Freud], 65
Quinn, A. H., 123

Rank, O., 2, 6
Rapaport, D., 27, 59, 88, 92
reality, 11–17, 20, 23
  delusional, 14, 17, 84, 89
  empirical, 24
  experiential, 20, 28, 31, 44
  external, 9, 10, 15, 38, 79, 80
  factual, 9
  Freud's conceptualizations of, 9
  internal, 61, 79
    vs. external, 17
  material, 9, 10, 11, 41, 56
  nature of, 9
  objective, 20, 24, 34
  omega indications of, 68
  perception of, 49–53
  principle, 35, 79
  psychic, 14, 41, 49, 50, 94
    and affect, 13
    concept of, 11, 21, 23, 34, 56
    of dynamic unconscious, 11, 26
    vs. external reality, 79
    lived experience of, 58, 60
    vs. material reality, 9, 10
    psychoanalysis as science of [Freud], 9, 10, 12
    of unconscious fantasy, 31
    of unconscious wish, 31
  sensual and psychic [Bion], 49
  testing, 24, 38, 39, 55, 117
  thought, 9
  unconscious, 12, 50, 79
  vs. wish-fulfilment, 23
regression, 97, 126
  formal [Freud], 93Reich, A., 4
Reich, W., 6, 96
Reichmayr, J., 4, 5
Reik, T., 4
representation, archaic (pre-logical) means of, 93
repression(s), 36, 37–44
  barrier, 15, 116, 117
  primal, 38
rigidity and openness, and character structure, 15, 115–118
resistance, 8, 98
  and character, 101
Richards, A., 1
Richardson, W. J., 120, 134
Ricoeur, P., 424
Rothman, S. M., 125
Roustang, F., 120
sadism, 112
  oral, 16, 126
Saling, M., 61
Sand, R., 53
Sandler, J., 2, 8, 46, 54, 59
Sartain, J., 131–132
Schafer, R., 3
Schilder, P., 84, 88, 92
schizophrenia(s), 13, 14, 43, 76, 83, 84, 92
  acute, 90
  chronic, 87, 89, 90–91
  hebephrenic–catatonic, 85
  perceptual anomalies in, 87–88
  pharmacological control of, 47
Schlesinger, H., 96–98, 100–101, 103
Schore, A., 60
Schur, M., 35
Schwartz, A., 46
Searle, J., 37, 40
secondary process, 9, 11, 14, 29, 33, 37, 41, 42, 117
  perception, 30
self-awareness vs. simple awareness, 49
self-psychological perspective, 3
serotonin uptake blockers, 47
sexual identity, 107
  and character, 101, 109–115
Sharrock, W. W., 1
Shengold, L., 98, 102, 115
Shevrin, H., 10, 19, 33, 39
signal theory [Freud], 5
Silverman, K., 119, 153
social psychology, psychoanalysis as, 1
Solms, M., x, xiii, 12–13, 17, 21, 45–81, 100
Solnit, A. J., x, xi–xiv, 98
Spelke, E., 40
Spitz, R., 36
Steiner, R., 2
Stekel, W., 2
Sterba, R. F., 4–8
Stern, D., 25–26, 36, 60
structural model of mind [Freud], 1–5, 8–9, 20, 33

sublimation, 100
substitution, 13, 85, 86, 92
superego, 57, 61, 99–102, 132
  childhood, 117
  development, 15
  –ego–id:
    relationship, 15
    structure, 9
symptom neuroses, 96, 97
synaesthesia, 55, 87, 92
syncretism, 92, 93

Tartakoff, H. H., 98
teeth, 16, 119–136
theft, 16, 119–136
thinking:
  pathological, 84–87
  theory of, 37
thioxanthenes, 47
thought:
  identity, 41
  reality, 9
topographical model, 2, 8, 10, 11, 13, 20, 21, 33, 65
transcendental ego, 30, 36
transference, 11, 27–31, 36, 43–44, 85
  and conscious experience, 27
  experiential mechanism of, 30
  Freud's theory of, 27–29
  function of, 29
  illusion, 44
  illusory experience of, 30
  interpretation of, 8
  need of unconscious for, 27, 30, 36
  operation of, 31, 43
  perceptual illusions of, 43
  principal aspects of, 27
  theory of anxiety [Freud], 5
  and unconscious fantasies, 27
transitivism, 14, 88, 92
trauma, reaction to, 102
tricyclics, 47
Turkle, S., 4
twin studies, 96, 97
Tyson, P., 114

unconscious, Freud's theory of, 21
unconscious mental processes, 9, 10, 13, 53, 83–94
unpleasure, 29, 34, 35, 47, 56– 60, 71, 73, 74
  and affect, 13
  and pleasure, pursuit of, 46
unpredictability, 105–106

Valenstein, A., 98–100
Van Essen, D., 69
Vienna Psycho-Analytical Society, 4, 6–7
Vienna Psychoanalytic Institute, 4, 6
Von Domarus, E., 43

Waelder, R., xii, 4, 6, 8, 96, 99
Wallerstein, R., 1, 3, 9, 96–97, 100, 107
Werner, H., 88, 92
Williams, W., 10
Winnicott, D. W., 30, 130
Wiseberg, S., 96, 97, 108
wish(es):
  -fulfilment:
    hallucinatory, 11, 21–28, 31, 33, 38, 117
    mode of, 34, 38
    reality-, 23
  mechanism of, 29
  primal, 35
  unconscious, 9, 11, 21, 22, 27–28, 31, 41–44
    mechanism of, 29

Yorke, C., x, xiii, 2, 3, 13–15, 17, 95–118
Young-Bruehl, E., 6

Zeki, S., 52, 67, 69

For Product Safety Concerns and Information please contact our EU representative GPSR@taylorandfrancis.com
Taylor & Francis Verlag GmbH, Kaufingerstraße 24, 80331 München, Germany

www.ingramcontent.com/pod-product-compliance
Lightning Source LLC
LaVergne TN
LVHW021108300926
849160LV00009B/654